High Performance Parallel Computing

Edited by Satyadhyan Chickerur

Published in London, United Kingdom

IntechOpen

Supporting open minds since 2005

High Performance Parallel Computing
http://dx.doi.org/10.5772/intechopen.73629
Edited by Satyadhyan Chickerur

Contributors
Hoon Ryu, Oh-Kyoung Kwon, Song Fu, Song Huang, Scott Pakin, Michael Lang, Koji Koyamada, Naohisa Sakamoto, Giuseppe Bilotta, Vito Zago, Alexis Hérault, Giorgos Vasiliadis, Satyadhyan Chickerur

First published in London, United Kingdom, 2019 by IntechOpen
IntechOpen is the global imprint of INTECHOPEN LIMITED, registered in England and Wales, registration number: 11086078, The Shard, 25th floor, 32 London Bridge Street
London, SE19SG – United Kingdom
Printed in Croatia

British Library Cataloguing-in-Publication Data
A catalogue record for this book is available from the British Library

Additional hard copies can be obtained from orders@intechopen.com

High Performance Parallel Computing
Edited by Satyadhyan Chickerur
p. cm.
Print ISBN 978-1-78985-623-1
Online ISBN 978-1-78985-624-8

For EU product safety concerns:
IN TECH d.o.o., Prolaz Marije Krucifikse Kozulić 3, 51000 Rijeka, Croatia, info@intechopen.com or visit our website at intechopen.com.

Meet the editor

Satyadhyan Chickerur has a BE degree in Electronics and Communications, MTech in CSE, and PhD in Computer and Information Sciences. He has served as Faculty in various engineering colleges in India. Presently, he is with the Department of Computer Science and Engineering, KLE Technological University (formerly BV Bhoomaraddi College of Engineering and Technology), Hubli, as a Professor and Head of the Centre for High Performance Computing. He is one of the members of the NVIDIA University Coordination Committee and is an NVIDIA DLI certified instructor. He is a member of ISTE, IEEE, and ACM. He was the Execom member of the IEEE Signal Processing Society, Bangalore chapter (2007–2009). He was a member of the Intel–IISC–VTU Multicore Curriculum Development Committee. Satyadhyan was one of the judges and a problem setter for the ACM ICPC programming contest of the Asia Regionals in 2007 and 2008. He has received various grants from industry and other organizations for research. The majority of the course offerings since 2007 were designed and developed based on the concept of outcome-based education, involving modified Bloom's taxonomy, project-based learning, and practice-based learning in collaboration/association with various industries. He has published his research papers in various journals and conferences, and has also presented tutorials and invited talks on various occasions. Additionally, he is a referee for various international journals and conferences. His research interests include image processing, soft computing, parallel and multicore programming, and communication systems. He received the BOLT award from Air India for 2008–2009. His biography has been profiled in *Marquis Who's Who in Science and Engineering* 2007 and in *Who's Who in the World* 2008, 2012, 2013, 2014, and 2016.

Contents

Preface

This edited book aims to present the state of the art in research and development of the convergence of high-performance computing and parallel programming for various applications. The book has consolidated algorithms and techniques to bridge the gap between the theoretical foundations of academia and implementation for research, which might be used in business applications in the future.

The book outlines techniques and tools used for emergent areas and domains, including acceleration of large-scale electronic structure simulations with heterogeneous parallel computing, characterizing power and energy efficiency of a data-centric HPC runtime and applications, security applications of GPUs, parallel implementation of multiprocessors on MPI using FDTD, particle-based fused rendering, design and implementation of particle systems for mesh-free methods with high performance, and evolving topics on heterogeneous computing.

It is certainly not an ambition to cover everything on HPPC in this book; rather this edited work features the latest methodologies, technical progress, and the direction in which the research is going.

The intended audience of this book will mainly consist of researchers, research students, and practitioners in the area of HPPC. I would like to convey my appreciation to all the contributors, including the accepted chapters' authors and many others who submitted their chapters but couldn't be included in the book due to various limitations.

My thanks to the editorial team, especially Mrs. Marina Dusevic, for their kind support and great efforts in publishing this book on time.

Satyadhyan Chickerur
KLE Technological University, Hubballi, India

Chapter 1

Introductory Chapter: High Performance Parallel Computing

Satyadhyan Chickerur

1. Introduction

High performance computing research had an interesting journey from the year 1972 to this day. In the initial years HPC was considered synonyms with supercomputing and was accessible to the scientists and researchers who worked in the domain of aeronautics, automobiles, petrochemicals, pharmaceuticals, particle physics, weather forecasting, etc. to name a few. Next came a phase where the term supercomputing gradually was replaced by high performance computing and the computing power gradually shifted to PCs in the form of multicore processors for various reasons. This was the time when lot of researchers saw benefit in parallelizing their applications achieving speedups, scale ups and robustness. This was possible because of concepts like Message passing interface, OpenMP, etc. which got evolved. Lot of research was carried out related to HPC systems architecture, computational models, parallel algorithms, and performance optimization, as a result of which renewed interest was created in parallel computing for HPC. This interest was also sustained because of:

I. Real time applications needed parallel processing for improving speedup.

II. Growing interest in artificial intelligence and machine learning.

III. Huge amount of data collected because of the revolution in the mobile industry.

The past decade has seen democratization of massively parallel computing with the introduction of accelerators in various forms, GPUs, and technologies like cloud computing, HPC, Big data, and web technologies converging. The extent to which we can parallelize an application/program depends on the granularity required. A program running on the system can be considered as a big task which can be split into smaller tasks and if these smaller tasks can be executed in parallel, then the parallel programming can be applied to achieve better performance. Because of the various new parallel architectures available, the developers now are in a better position to decide whether they want the application to be coarse grained or fine grained. The next decade will see a rise in the applications related to computer vision, image and video processing, machine and deep learning, web services, natural language processing, medicine, drug discovery, autonomous driving, and biotechnology.

The research/application development today aims to solve the real world problems in the area of healthcare, automobiles, weather, security, etc. The chapters in this edited volume try to capture few of the recent research work in related areas.

2. Conclusions

The next decade will see the convergence of high performance computing and massively parallel computing for various applications and will help the researchers and scientists to solve problems which few years back were thought to be unsolvable.

Acknowledgements

The editor would like to acknowledge the support of the management of K LE Technological University during the duration of the editing of this book. This edition would not have been released on time without the support of the editorial team of IntechOpen, especially the Author Service Manager, Mrs. Marina Dusevic.

Author details

Satyadhyan Chickerur
KLE Technological University, Hubballi, India

*Address all correspondence to: chickerursr@kletech.ac.in

Chapter 2

Acceleration of Large-Scale Electronic Structure Simulations with Heterogeneous Parallel Computing

Oh-Kyoung Kwon and Hoon Ryu

Abstract

Large-scale electronic structure simulations coupled to an empirical modeling approach are critical as they present a robust way to predict various quantum phenomena in realistically sized nanoscale structures that are hard to be handled with density functional theory. For tight-binding (TB) simulations of electronic structures that normally involve multimillion atomic systems for a direct comparison to experimentally realizable nanoscale materials and devices, we show that graphical processing unit (GPU) devices help in saving computing costs in terms of time and energy consumption. With a short introduction of the major numerical method adopted for TB simulations of electronic structures, this work presents a detailed description for the strategies to drive performance enhancement with GPU devices against traditional clusters of multicore processors. While this work only uses TB electronic structure simulations for benchmark tests, it can be also utilized as a practical guideline to enhance performance of numerical operations that involve large-scale sparse matrices.

Keywords: offload computing, GPU devices, large-scale electronic structure simulations, tight-binding approach, nanoelectronics modeling

1. Introduction

As the dimension of functional semiconductor devices are scaled down to deca-nanometer (nm) sizes, the underlying material can no longer be considered continuous. The number of atoms in the active device region becomes countable in the range of ~50 K to a few millions, and their local arrangements in interfaces, alloys, and strained systems give non-negligible effects on device characteristics [1–3]. Also, most experimentally realized structures are not infinitely periodic, but are finite in sizes; such geometries call for a local orbital basis, rather than a plane wave basis which implies infinite periodicity. As full *ab-initio* methods such as density functional theory are in principle hard to simulate electronic structures of such a huge and discrete atomic structures [4, 5], the necessity of atomistic approaches based on an empirical modeling method is quite huge.

The *spds** 10-band tight-binding (TB) approach, which employs a set of 10 localized orbital bases to describe a single atom, has been extensively used to explain experimental behaviors of various quantum devices [2, 6–9] through large-scale electronic structure simulations with the well-known nanoelectronics modeling tool (NEMO) [10, 11]. As the NEMO only runs in traditional computing clusters of multicore processors, we also have recently released a new software package for TB simulations (Quantum simulation tool for Advanced Nanoscale Devices (Q-AND)), which supports computation with Intel Xeon Phi PCI-E add-in devices and shows enhanced performance compared to the result obtained with clusters of Intel Xeon multicore processors [12].

The major purpose of this work is to explore the performance benefits that can be obtained with NVIDIA general-purpose graphical processing unit (GPU) devices, which are also PCI-E add-in devices and are popularly adopted by communities to solve various computing-intensive problems. In particular, (1) we present methodological details applied to enhance the performance of TB electronic structure simulations with GPU devices. Then (2) we show the excellence of speed and scalability for end-to-end simulations of realistically sized nanostructures and (3) analyze the economic benefits of latest GPU devices for TB simulations against computing resources of multicore processors (host CPUs). Extending our previous work with Intel Knights Corner coprocessors [12] to the area of GPU computing, this work delivers practical information for technical details that are employed to accelerate empirical modeling of large-scale electronic structures and therefore can serve as a guideline that is beneficial to researchers in the field of nanoelectronics who consider a code migration to heterogeneous computing platforms involving PCI-E communications, which takes a non-negligible portion of top 500 high-performance computing systems in the world [13]. While latest NVIDIA GPU devices also support NVLink communications, here we only consider the PCI-E one for the performance analysis.

2. Methodology

Electronic structures of target nanostructures are described with a $sp^3d^5s^*$ TB model [6, 9, 10], which employs 10 orthogonal orbital bases to represent a single atom assuming nearest-neighbor couplings. As shown in **Figure 1** (top), simulation domains are decomposed in a multidimensional manner with MPI and OpenMP. Hamiltonian matrices, which are stored in compressed sparse row (CSR) format [14], are then decomposed in a row-wise manner. The Schrödinger equation solver, which computes normal eigenvalue problems in a numerical perspective, is developed with the Lanczos method [15] whose computational bottleneck comes from sparse matrix-vector multiplication (SpMV) [12, 15]. The basic idea for the performance improvement would thus be to perform SpMV with a simultaneous utilization of host CPUs and GPU devices, where **Figure 1** (bottom) illustrates this idea. Here, each GPU device has a block matrix belonging to an MPI process, which sends/receives input (Vin)/output (Vout) vectors to/from the associated GPU device. Each MPI process does not need to send the whole Vin since multiplication in an MPI process can be done with only three block vectors of Vin (1 in itself, 2 in its neighbor processes) as our TB model assumes nearest-neighbor couplings. Upon the completion of multiplication, a GPU device just needs to send 1 block of Vout) back to its associated MPI process. Host CPUs and GPU devices can thus perform multiplication simultaneously with no heavy overhead of data transfer. In the next subsections, we present further detailed methodologies for (1) the simultaneous utilization of host CPUs and GPU devices and (2) the implementation of efficient SpMV CUDA kernels.

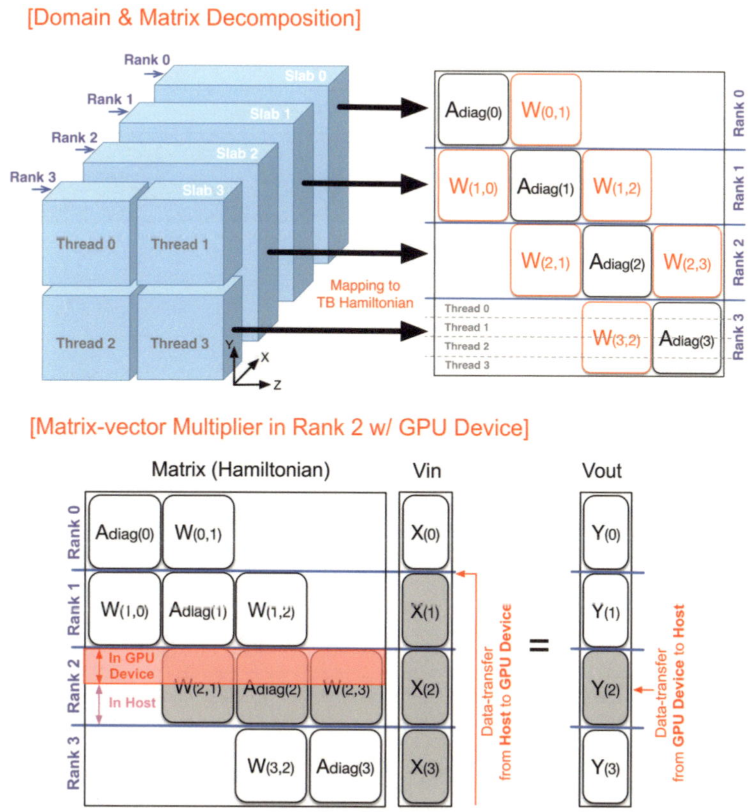

Figure 1.
(Top) scheme for domain decomposition. Hamiltonian matrices representing real-space simulation domains are decomposed in a row-wise manner with a hybrid use of MPI and OpenMP. (bottom) conceptual illustration of how to share the computing load of matrix-vector multiplication into both host CPUs and GPU devices.

2.1 Simultaneous utilization of both CPU and GPU

The following are two ways of how to efficiently utilize the resources of both CPUs and GPUs. One takes the pageable memory when transferring data between CPU and GPU, whereas the other uses the pinned memory. The memory can be allocated in the pinned memory with the *cudaMallocHost* function of CUDA library, which prevents the memory from being paged out and therefore improves the speed of data transfer between host and GPU devices. The pageable (non-pinned) memory can be used with the *malloc* function of standard C library. This subsession will discuss in detail how SpMV can be done with the abovementioned two ways.

Computations of SpMV in host CPU and GPU devices are overlapped in default since the GPU kernel function is called in a non-blocking manner such that its execution can be done in parallel with the execution in CPU code. As shown in **Figure 2(a)**, however, data transfer between host and (GPU) device memory cannot be overlapped with the CPU computation when the pageable memory is used. As depicted in **Figure 2(b)**, the pinned memory enables the CPU calculation to be overlapped with data transfer [16]. Another merit that can be obtained with the pinned memory is that the effective bandwidth of data transfer itself is increased by ~3 times compared to the one obtained with the pageable memory, because the bandwidth of the PCI-E bus to connect CPU and GPU is not fully exploited with the pageable memory [16]. The pinned memory can be used with the *cudaMallocHost* (CUDA library) instead of *malloc* function. As memory offload is much faster and

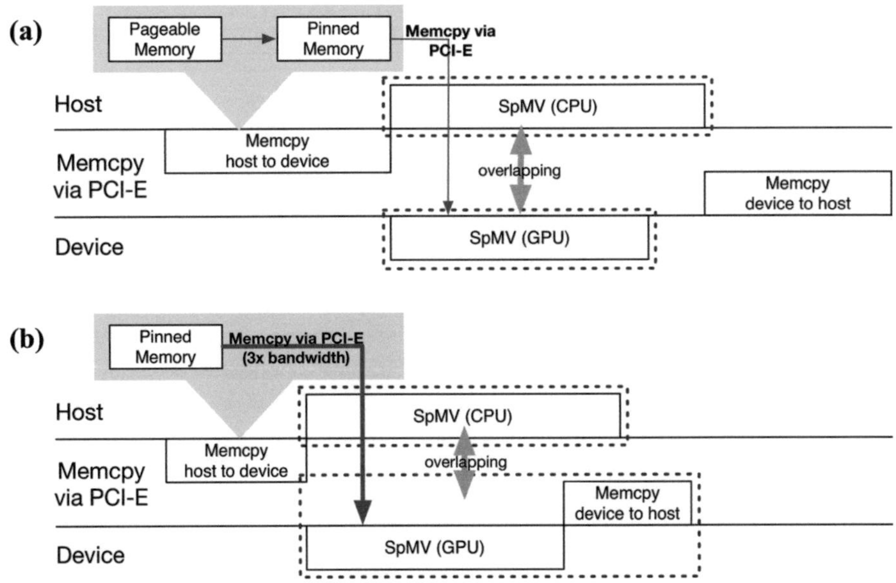

Figure 2.
Comparison of two methodologies for simultaneous utilization of both CPU and GPU. (a) With pageable memory, data transfer between CPUs and GPU devices cannot be hidden behind the SpMV computation. (b) With pinned memory, data transfer can be overlapped with the SpMV computation and can be performed with much higher bandwidth.

communication hiding is possible, the pinned memory would be superior to the page memory for saving the wall time of SpMV calculations with GPU devices.

2.2 CUDA SpMV kernels

We have developed three different CUDA SpMV kernels as illustrated in **Figure 3**: (i) a basic kernel that allocates a single CUDA thread per a row in the matrix (*naïve*), (ii) a kernel that always allocates a single WARP to the SPMV operation for a single row in the matrix (*warp1*) [17], and (iii) a kernel that dynamically allocates multiple WARPs to the SPMV operation for a single row in the matrix (*warp2*) [18].

Firstly, the *naive* kernel is a straightforward approach to map a single CUDA thread to a single row in the matrix. Because the Q-AND code uses the CSR format to describe the Hamiltonian matrix, SpMV operations need an indirect addressing step for every single scalar operation needed for multiplications. Consecutive threads therefore have to access irregularly strided memory as illustrated in **Figure 3(a)**. As noted by Harris [19], such access patterns would degrade performance, because then successive threads may not be able to access the global memory simultaneously to read non-zero elements of the matrix (**Figure 3(a)**).

Secondly, the *warp1* kernel uses the maximum number of CUDA threads of a single WARP for multiplications of a single row in the matrix. A WARP is defined as the group of threads and consists of contiguous threads (32 threads for Tesla K40 devices) [19, 20]. Since threads in a single WARP can access the global memory simultaneously, we can reduce the number of transactions that are required to access the global memory, and therefore we expect non-negligible performance enhancement for SpMV operations against the *naïve* kernel (**Figure 3(b)**) [18]. However, this solution may not be the best one, since we always use a single WARP for a single matrix row, and therefore we may have idle threads (or WARPs) if the maximum number of WARPs supported by a single GPU device is larger than the number of rows of a block matrix that are belonging to that GPU device.

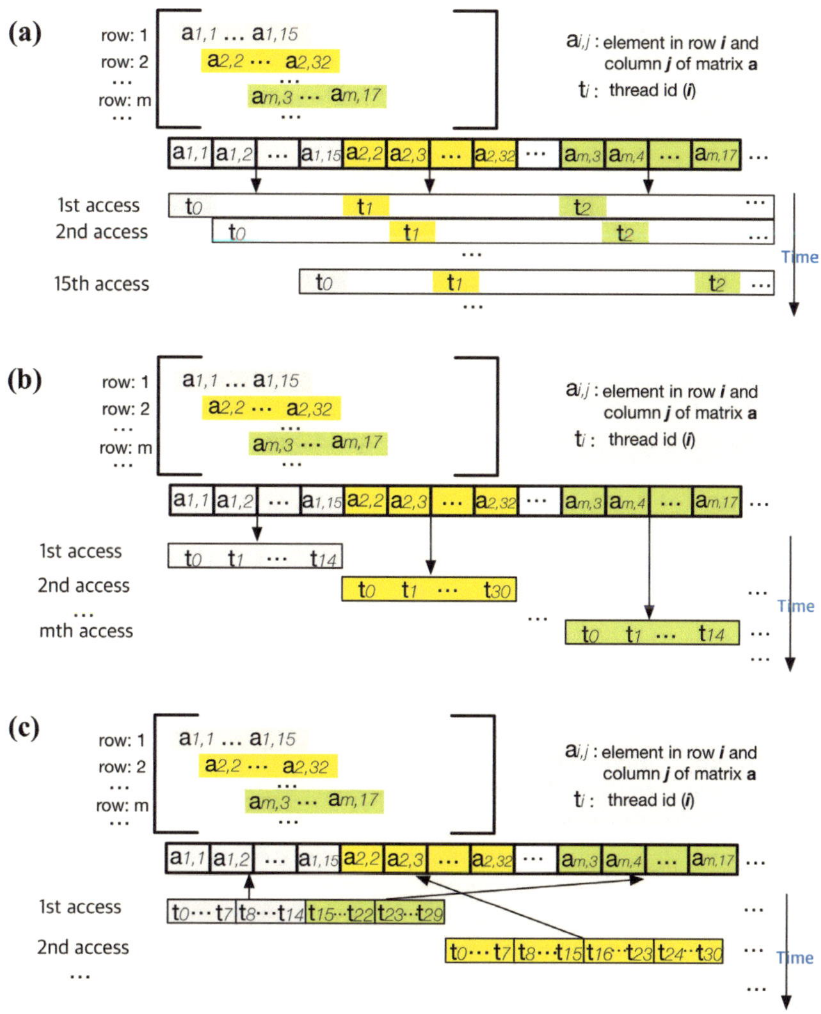

Figure 3.
Conceptual scheme of three SpMV CUDA kernels. (a) A basic kernel that maps a single thread to a single row in the matrix for SpMV (naive). Here, consecutive threads (t_0, t_1,…,t_{n-1}) access nonconsecutive words. (b) A kernel that uses WARP statically (warp1). It always allocates a single WARP (32 threads in Tesla K40) to a single row in the matrix. Consecutive threads (t_0, t_1,…,t_{n-1}) access consecutive words. (c) A kernel that uses WARP dynamically (warp2). It dynamically allocates WARPs to a single row considering the sparsity of matrix.

Thirdly, the *warp2* kernel dynamically allocates WARPs to a single matrix row as depicted in **Figure 3(c)**. Here, the number of WARPs allocated to a single matrix row is dynamically determined by counting the number of corresponding non-zero elements, i.e., an integer value that is closest to "the number of non-zero elements in one matrix row/the number of threads per a single WARP. "We note the *warp2* kernel would be optimal for our problem since the TB Hamiltonian matrix normally has non-zero elements that are larger than 32.

In addition, we can increase the performance by utilizing the texture memory for the vector data retrieval, where texture memory, which is a read-only memory, is cached on-chip and provides higher effective bandwidth by reducing memory requests toward off-chip DRAM. Since the in/out vectors are irregularly accessed by threads from the global memory of GPU devices, the performance improvement could be driven by applying the texture memory. The following section reveals the result of the evaluation.

3. Results and discussions

This section discusses the performance evaluation of our solver from following perspectives: (i) the strong/weak scalability of end-to-end simulations and the optimal *GPU load* (i.e., the portion of SpMV calculation allocated to GPU devices that shows the best speed), (ii) impact of the pinned memory on computing performance, (iii) performances of the three different CUDA SpMV kernels, and (iv) energy efficiency and economic benefit of GPU computing for electronic structure simulations against the results obtained with CPU computing only. All the benchmark tests are performed on the two test-bed machines: one is the K40 test-bed including three computing nodes connected with an infinite-band 4 × FDR (56 Gbps) network, where each node has two Intel Xeon CPUs E5-2650 v3 [21], two NVIDIA Tesla K40 GPU cards [20], and one 128G DDR3 1867 MHz memory, and another is a P100 test-bed including one node with same configuration except two NVIDIA Tesla P100 cards [22]. The codes are compiled with CUDA 8.0 library, Intel C++ compiler 16.0, and OpenMPI 1.10.2. Si:P quantum dots (QDs), which are defined to be huge silicon (Si) layers encapsulating a single phosphorus (P) atom and are studied with a 10-band TB model for designs of Si-based quantum computers [8, 9, 23], are used as target devices for all the benchmark tests.

3.1 Evaluation of utilization of both GPUs and CPUs

Using the pinned memory and the *warp2* kernel with texture memory, simulations are performed for Si:P QDs with a convergence criterion of 10^{-8} eV and are completed when 10^4 Lanczos iterations are reached or 10 lowest energy levels in conduction band are found. Every bar graph of **Figure 4** has the following six elements: MPI communication (*Comm*), data transfer from host to GPU device (*CopyIn*), SpMV + data transfer from GPU device to host (*SpMV + CopyOut*), dot product (*VVDot*), memory operations (*MemOp*), and other portions (*Others*). Note that *SpMV + CopyOut* includes the time required for SpMV on GPU devices and data transfer from GPU device to host memory, while SpMV on CPUs is performed at the same time.

Figure 4(a) and **(b)** presents the strong and weak scalability of the end-to-end simulation at the K40 and P100 test-beds, respectively. The Si:P QD tested for the strong scalability has a cuboid Si layer that consists of a total of 30 × 80 × 80 [100] unit cells and has a dimension of ~16 nm × 43 nm × 43 nm (about 1.5 million atoms). The problem size for the weak scalability test is 15n × 80 × 80 [100] unit cells (n × 7.5 × 10^5 atoms), where n denotes the number of MPI ranks. As we use 10 bases to describe a single atom, the degrees of freedom (DOF) of corresponding Hamiltonian matrices are ~15 million (for strong scalability) and ~7.5 million/rank (for weak scalability), respectively. Here, we see that the strong scalability is generally quite good, where each MPI rank is mapped to 10 CPU cores and one GPU card. The job using six MPI ranks is 2.34 times faster than the one executed with two ranks for the 30 × 80 × 80 unitcells at the K40 test-bed. It shows nice scales according to the number of cores, because a significant portion of the wall time is taken by SpMV that would give a nice scalability as the matrix has a block-tridiagonal shape, and therefore the burden of MPI communications would not become a serious problem. The weak scalability also shows good since the wall time is not significantly affected by MPI communications.

In addition, **Figure 4(c)** and **(d)** illustrates the performance comparison in terms of the wall time according to the GPU load at the K40 and P100 test-beds,

DOI: http://dx.doi.org/10.5772/intechopen.80997

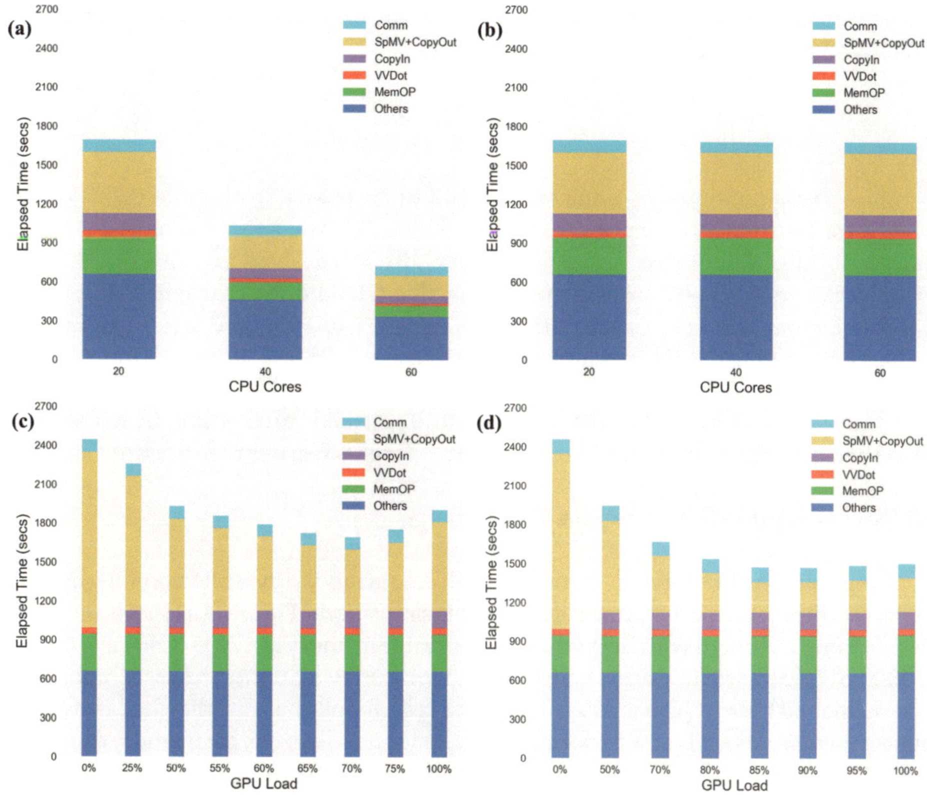

Figure 4.
Performance of Q-AND code with GPUs computing using the pinned memory and the warp2 kernel with texture memory. (a) Strong scalability of computing 30 × 80 × 80 unit cells at the K40 test-bed. (b) Weak scalability of computing 15 × 80 × 80 unit cells per single MPI process at the K40 test-bed. (c) Performance of computing 30 × 80 × 80 unit cells as a function of the GPU load at the K40 test-bed. (d) Performance comparison of computing 30 × 80 × 80 unit cells as a function of the GPU load at the P100 test-bed.

respectively. The QD considered for the experiment here has 30 × 80 × 80 unit cells. The elapsed time is described as a function of computing load for SpMV on GPU devices (GPU load). As described in the previous section, SpMV is the most time-consuming part such that it takes about 56% of the wall time when CPUs perform all the multiplications (*GPU load* is zero) at the K40 test-bed. However, as the GPU load increases, SpMV takes less time and shows the best speed when the GPU load is ~70%. This *optimal* GPU load depends on the hardware performance of GPU devices such that, at the P100 test-bed (with same host CPUs), it is ~90%. The speedup becomes 1.44× and 1.7× for the target simulation at the K40 and P100 test-beds, respectively, against the case when GPU load is zero (only CPUs are used for simulations).

Then let us discuss why this optimal GPU load becomes about 70 and 90% at the K40 and P100 test-beds, respectively. Since the performance of SpMV depends on various factors such as computing units, memory bandwidth and latency, network speed, and PCI-E bandwidth between host and GPU device, it is not easy to clearly extract the exact value of the optimal GPU load. However, the "ideal value" of the *GPU load* could be approximately calculated using only the theoretical peak performance of computing units, because the performance of SpMV would be maximized when both CPUs and GPUs complete computing operations at the same time. If we denote the peak performance (in the unit of floating point operations per second (FLOPS)) of host CPUs and PCI-E connected devices by P_H and P_D, respectively, the optimal GPU load (x) can be calculated as the following equation (Eq. (1)):

$$x = \frac{100 \times P_D}{P_D + P_H} \quad (1)$$

Since a single computing node of the K40 test-bed has a P_H of about 0.736×10^{12} FLOPS for twenty CPU cores of Xeon E5-2650 v3 [21], and a P_D of about 2.620×10^{12} FLOPS for two Tesla K40 devices [20], x is derived to about 78.1%, which it is a little higher than the measured value (70%) due to the ignorance of other factors (memory bandwidth, etc.). For the P100 test-bed (P_D of about 10.600×10^{12} FLOPS) [22], x is also evaluated to about 93.5%, while we find it at ~90%. Even though the derived values are not strictly accurate, we can still explain why the optimal GPU load of the K40 and P100 test-beds turns out to be higher than the one (~65%) measured with Xeon Phi Knights Corner coprocessors [12].

3.2 Effects of pinned memory on performance

As explained in the previous section, the pinned memory may make a non-negligible impact on the overall performance of large-scale simulations. **Figure 5(a)** shows the performance measured with the pinned and pageable memory at a 70% (K40) and 90% (P100) GPU load, where a single computing node is used with the *warp2* kernel and texture memory. The Si:P QD has 30 × 80 × 80 unit cells. Results indicate that the case with pinned memory shows better performance than the one with pageable memory due to the following two points: (1) The reduction of *CopyIn* time due to the increased bandwidth of PCI-E bus with pinned memory and (2) *SpMV* + *CopyOut* time as communication hiding behind the computation. We observed the effective bandwidth of PCI-E communication is ~3.31 GB/s with the pageable memory on every test-bed, while it reaches ~10.40 GB/s with the pinned memory, driving ~3.14 speedup in data transfer. The effective speed of SpMV operations increases by a factor of 1.36 and 1.19 with pinned memory compared to the speed with pageable memory at the K40 and P100 test-beds, respectively, since utilization of the pinned can overlap computation and data transfer. The performance for end-to-end simulations therefore becomes 1.27 and 1.21 times faster with pinned memory against the performance obtained with pageable memory at 70% GPU load (K40) and 90% GPU load (P100), respectively.

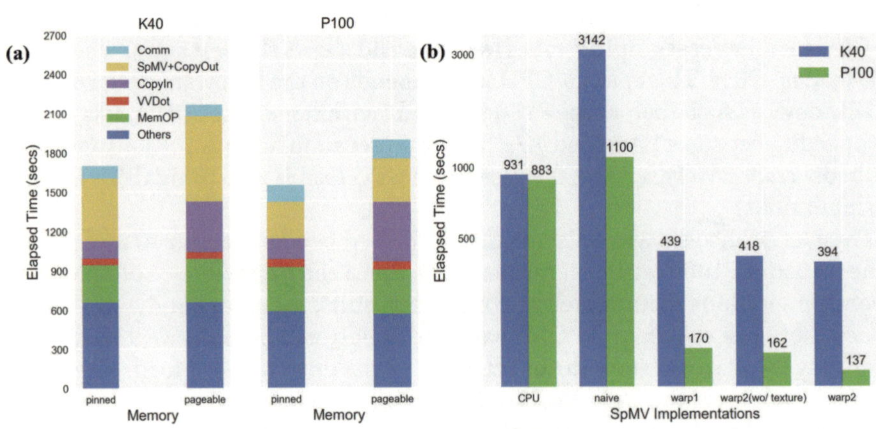

Figure 5.
Performance measured in a single computing node for end-to-end simulations of 30 × 80 × 80 unit cells at the optimal GPU load (70% for K40 and 90% for P100). (a) Performance measured with the pinned and pageable memory when the warp2 kernel is used. (b) Performance of three different SpMV CUDA implementations. SPMV calculations are slightly accelerated with utilization of the texture memory.

Though here we only focused on the performance of PCI-E communications, it is possible to estimate the performance benefit that may be obtained with NVLink communications. For this purpose, we investigate how the bandwidth of communications between CPU and GPU affects the overall performance, where we find that the overall speedup is ~1.21× due to the ~3.1× enhancement of PCI-E bandwidth on the effects of pinned memory in PCI-E add-in P100 devices. Because the bandwidth improvement with NVLink connectivity between CPU and GPU is ~3× compared to the PCI-E [24], we may roughly expect that there will be another ~1.06× speedup for the end-to-end simulation with NVLink add-in P100 devices.

3.3 Performance analysis of SpMV CUDA kernels

Here we investigate the performance of three different SpMV CUDA kernels and present a short discussion about the effects of the texture memory on the performance. **Figure 5(b)** shows the performance of the three SpMV implementations at the single computing node of the K40 and P100 test-beds, where the pinned memory is utilized with a 70% (K40) and 90% (P100) GPU load. The Si:P QD for target simulations has 30 × 80 × 80 unit cells. The grid/block size is set to 21,000/256 and 672,000/256 of the *naive* and *warp1* kernel, respectively. For the *warp2* kernel, the grid/block size is set to 30/1024 and 112/1024 at the K40 and P100 test-beds, respectively, since the number of streaming multiprocessors is 56 for P100 devices, while it is 15 for K40 (the grid size is set to an integer multiple of the number of available streaming multiprocessors).

Among the *naive*, *warp1*, and *warp2* kernel, the *warp2* outperforms as expected. The speedup of the *warp2* kernel is the 7.96/6.73 (K40/P100) and 1.12/1.24 compared to the *naive* and the *warp1* kernel, respectively. The huge performance enhancement that is particularly achieved against the *naive* kernel reflects the importance of coalescing global memory access as Liu et al. also reported that the effective bandwidth is poor for large strided memory access [18]. The *warp2* kernel also works faster than the *warp1* kernel since less threads would be idle with dynamic allocations as discussed in the "Methodology" section. While multiple WARPs can be involved to process a single row in the matrix (and threads in a single WARP can concurrently access the global memory), there is an inter-WARP time lag (only a single WARP can process multiplications at a time). The performance gain, however, is remarkable such that 15–20% of the wall time is reduced with a dynamic allocation of WARPs.

All the three kernels show faster operations in P100 devices than in K40 devices, and the speedup in P100 devices turns out to be ~2.77 on average. Although the peak performance of P100 devices is 4.05× higher than that of K40 devices (in FLOPS for double precision), the measured average performance gain (2.77) is much lower than this value (4.05), since the performance of SpMV is mainly limited by the bandwidth of global memory rather than the core clock of GPU devices [25]. **Figure 5(b)** also shows the performance difference created by utilization of the texture memory for retrieval of vector data retrieval. With the texture memory, the speed of the *warp2* kernel improves by a factor of 1.06 (K40) and 1.19 (P100) against the case without the texture memory, since the texture memory enables fast random accesses to vector data and uses a cache to provide broad bandwidth.

3.4 Energy efficiency and economic benefits of GPU computing

Not only is the elapsed time an important metric, but also the energy efficiency is a significant one to explore. The power usage of host and the two PCI-E connected devices is evaluated as a function of elapsed time (**Figure 6**), where we consider the power consumed by host (CPU packages with off-chip DRAMs) and Tesla GPU devices. The power usage in host and GPU devices is measured with Intel Running Average Power Limit (RAPL) library [26] and NVIDIA Management Library (NVML) [27], respectively.

Figure 6(a), (b) and **(c)** shows the real-time power consumption of a single computing node at a 0% GPU load (CPU only), 70% GPU load with K40, and 90% GPU load with P100 GPU devices, respectively. A Si:P QD consisting of 30 × 80 × 80 unit cells is simulated with the *warp2* kernel where pinned memory and texture memory are used. Here, all the results show similar patterns such that *(i)* the power consumption starts to increase during the initial processes of electronic structure simulations, i.e., matrix construction that requires memory access to store non-zero elements, row/column indices. *(ii)* The power usage then shows a rapid oscillation during the process of Lanczos iterations, and *(iii)* it finally returns to the normal (standby) value when all the calculation is finished. **Figure 6(d)** informs that the average instantaneous power consumption of a single computing node with K40 and P100 devices is 157.58 and 117.55 Watt, whereas the host of test-beds uses 279.76 and 270.05 Watt, respectively. **Figure 6(e)** shows the total energy consumed by the end-to-end simulation, which can be calculated by multiplying the time-averaged power usage by the wall time. During the execution in a single computing node of the K40 test-bed, CPUs and GPUs consume about 542.32 and 305.40 KJ, respectively, while corresponding values with P100 devices become 331.44 and 144.33 KJ, respectively. ~614.18KJ is consumed for the CPU-only case. Compared to the results measured with K40 GPU devices, a single computing node with P100 devices consumes ~1.34× less energy, while it finishes the target simulation ~2.88× faster. **Figure 6(f)** shows the total energy consumed by the three SpMV kernels in the single computing node of the K40 and P100 test-beds, where the pinned memory is utilized with a 70% (K40) and 90% (P100) GPU load for simulations of a Si:P QD consisting of 30 × 80 × 80 unit cells. Coalescence of global memory access (**Figure 3(c)**) drives a significant performance improvement, such that the *warp2* kernel not only shows the smallest energy consumption but

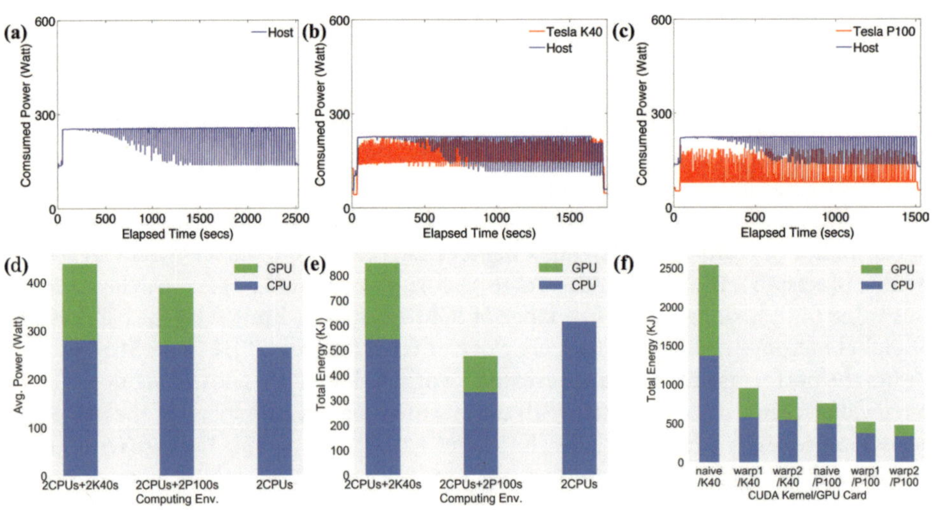

Figure 6.
Power usage and energy consumption associated with the target simulation. The real-time power consumption measured in a single computing node at (a) 0% GPU load (CPU only), (b) 70% GPU load with K40 devices, and (c) 90% GPU load with P100 devices. (d) Time-averaged power usage and (e) total energy consumption measured in a single computing node at the optimal GPU load (70% for K40 and 90% for P100). (f) Total energy consumption of three different SpMV CUDA implementations in a single computing node at the optimal GPU load.

has the best wall-time performance among the three kernels. Reduction in energy consumption of the *warp2* kernel turns out to be 2.99×/1.59× (K40/P100) and 1.12×/1.09× compared to the *naive* and the *warp1* kernel, respectively.

Now let us talk about the energy efficiency of our code for electronic structure simulations. Without losing generality, we roughly can define the energy efficiency as the rate of SpMV operations performed for the unit power consumption (1 W). The rate of SpMV operations can be estimated by the ratio of the total number of floating point operations that a single simulation performs (NF) and the total wall time taken until the simulation is completed. Therefore, the energy efficiency of simulations (η) can be approximated with Eq. (2):

$$\eta = \frac{NF}{T_{total}} \times \frac{1}{W} = \frac{NF}{E_{total}} \tag{2}$$

where E_{total} and T_{total} represent the total energy consumption and wall time required to complete a single simulation, respectively. From the derived equation, the energy efficiency could be calculated for K40 and P100 devices and host CPUs. Although it is not easy to exactly quantify NF, we can at least compare the energy efficiency of different computing devices by assuming that NF would be linearly proportional to the workload of SpMV allocated to specific computing platforms. By setting the energy efficiency of CPU-only computing to 1, the energy efficiency of K40 devices (70% GPU load) and P100 devices (90% GPU load) would be ~1.43 and 3.81, respectively. We conclude the energy efficiency of P100 devices is ~2.66× and 3.81× better than that of K40 and CPU devices for the target simulation. Note that these quantities are hard to be obtained just with officially known hardware specifications [20–22].

Finally, let us close this section with a short discussion about the economic benefits that can be delivered by GPU computing for TB simulations. Since GPU devices are not cheap [28, 29], it would be interesting to compare the "time saving" achieved by a single US dollar spent for additional GPU devices. As we already have shown in **Figure 4**, the CPU-only simulation of 30 × 80 × 80 unit cells is finished in ~2476 s, which is average of the results measured with K40 and P100 devices (**Figure 5(c)** and **(d)**). While the simulation is finished in ~1701 s with K40 at the optimal GPU load (70%), we must additionally pay ~4.6 K US dollars to buy two K40 GPU devices [28]. With P100 devices, the simulation takes ~1472 s at the optimal GPU load (90%) and requires ~14.7 K US dollars to buy two P100 GPU devices [29]. Thereby, we get ~0.17 and ~0.07 s/USD for K40 and P100 devices, respectively. While the performance enhancement driven by GPU computing may be impressive in the perspective of computing time, we claim more expensive devices may not always deliver better economic benefits. Readers are therefore strongly encouraged to build a careful budget plan whether they are thinking to buy new GPU devices.

4. Conclusion

The cost efficiency of general-purpose graphical processing unit (GPU) devices for tight-binding (TB) simulations of extremely large-scale electronic structures has been examined with a focus on the speed and the amount of energy consumption. Technical strategies used to exploit the strength of GPU-coupled offload computing have been elaborated in detail with a short but clear description of the main numerical method employed to tackle large-scale Schrödinger equations. Benchmark tests have been performed against realistically sized solid Si:P quantum dot devices that contain several million atoms. Tesla K40 and latest P100 GPU devices are considered as the test platform. The technics we employed for the efficient offload computing of large-scale TB simulations drive a non-negligible enhancement of the computing speed. Compared to the performance tested with Intel Xeon V3 host CPU only, K40 and P100 devices can achieve up to ~2× and ~6× speedup for sparse matrix-vector multiplication (SpMV), which is the numerical operation needed to solve electronic structures. In terms of the amount of total energy consumption, however, K40 shows worse performance compared to the CPU-only case, while P100 still holds the strength.

Acknowledgements

This work has been carried out as Intel Parallel Computing Centre (IPCC) project under the financial support from Intel Corporation, USA. Authors acknowledge the extensive use of KISTI Accelerator Test-bed (KAT) computing resources that are supported by Korea Institute of Science and Technology Information.

Author details

Oh-Kyoung Kwon† and Hoon Ryu*†
Korea Institute of Science and Technology Information, Daejeon, Republic of Korea

*Address all correspondence to: elec1020@kisti.re.kr

† These authors contributed equally.

References

[1] Shinada T, Okamoto S, Kobayashi T, Ohdomari I. Enhancing semiconductor device performance using ordered dopant arrays. Nature. 2005;**437**:1128-1131

[2] Usman M, Ryu H, Woo I, Ebert DS, Klimeck G. Moving toward Nano-TCAD through multimillion-atom quantum-dot simulations matching experimental data. IEEE Transactions on Nanotechnology. 2009;**8**:330-344

[3] Lee S, Ryu H, Campbell H, Hollenberg LCL, Simmons MY, Klimeck G. Electronic structure of realistically extended atomistically resolved disordered Si:P δ-doped layers. Physical Review B. 2011;**84**:205309

[4] Carter DJ, Warschkow O, Marks NA, McKenzi DR. Electronic structure models of phosphorus δ-doped silicon. Physical Review B. 2009;**79**:033204

[5] Carter DJ, Marks NA, Warschkow O, McKenzi DR. Phosphorus δ-doped silicon: Mixed-atom pseudopotentials and dopant disorder effects. Nanotechnology. 2011;**22**:1-10

[6] Ryu H, Lee S, Weber B, Mahapatra S, Hollenberg LCL, Simmons MY, et al. Atomistic modeling of metallic nanowires in silicon. Nanoscale. 2013;**5**:8666-8674

[7] Weber B, Mahapatra S, Ryu H, Lee S, Fuhrer A, Reusch TCG, et al. Ohm's law survives to the atomic scale. Science. 2012;**335**:64-67

[8] Ryu H, Lee S, Fuechsle M, Miwa JA, Mahapatra S, Hollenberg L, et al. A tight-binding study of single-atom transistors. Small. 2015;**11**:374-381

[9] Fuechsle M, Miwa JA, Mahapatra S, Ryu H, Lee S, Warschkow O, et al. A single-atom transistor. Nature Nanotechnology. 2012;7:242-246

[10] Klimeck G, Shahid Ahmed S, Bae H, Kharche N, Clark S, Haley B, et al. Atomistic simulation of realistically sized nanodevices using NEMO 3-D—Part I: Models and benchmarks. IEEE Transactions on Electron Devices. 2007;**54**:2079-2089

[11] Lee S, Ryu H, Jiang Z, Klimeck G. Million atom electronic structure and device calculations on peta-scale computers. In: Proceedings of 13th International Workshop on Computational Electronics (IWCE). 2009. pp. 1-4. DOI: 10.1109/IWCE.2009.5091117

[12] Ryu H, Jeong Y, Kang J-H, Cho KN. Q-AND: Time-efficient modelling of tight-binding electronic structures with many-core computing. Computer Physics Communications. 2016;**209**:79-87. DOI: 10.1016/j.cpc.2016.08.015

[13] Top 500 Supercomputer Sites. Available from: https://www.top500.org/ [Accessed: 03-04-2018]

[14] Buluç A, Fineman JT, Frigo M, Gilbert JR, Leiserson CE. Parallel sparse matrix-vector and matrix-transpose-vector multiplication using compressed sparse blocks. In: Proceedings of the Annual Symposium on Parallelism in Algorithms and Architectures (SPAA). 2009. pp. 233-244. DOI: 10.1145/1583991.1584053

[15] Lanczos C. An iteration method for the solution of the eigenvalue problem of linear differential and integral operators. Journal of Research of the National Bureau of Standards. 1950;**45**:255-282

[16] Harris M. How to Optimize Data Transfers in CUDA C/C++, NVIDIA PARALLEL FORALL. 2012. Available from: https://devblogs.nvidia.com/parallelforall/how-optimize-data-transfers-cuda-cc/ [Accessed: 02-03-2018]

[17] Bell N, Garland M. Efficient Sparse Matrix-Vector Multiplication on CUDA, NVIDIA Technical Report NVR-2008-004. 2008

[18] Liu Y, Schmidt B. LightSpMV: Faster CSR-based sparse matrix-vector multiplication on CUDA-enabled GPUs. In: 26th IEEE International Conference on Application-specific Systems, Architectures and Processors (ASAP 2015). 2015. pp. 82-89

[19] Harris M. How to Access Global Memory Efficiently in CUDA C/C++ Kernels, NVIDIA PARALLEL FORALL. 2013. Available from: https://devblogs.nvidia.com/parallelforall/how-access-global-memory-efficiently-cuda-c-kernels/ [Accessed: 02-03-2018]

[20] NVIDIA Tesla K40 GPU Accelerator. Available from: http://www.nvidia.com/content/PDF/kepler/Tesla-K40-PCIe-Passive-Board-Spec-BD-06902-001_v05.pdf [Accessed: 02-03-2018]

[21] Intel Xeon Processor E5-2650 v3. Available from: https://ark.intel.com/products/81705/Intel-Xeon-Processor-E5-2650-v3-25M-Cache-2_30-GHz. [Accessed: 02-03-2018]

[22] Whitepaper of NVIDIA Tesla P100 GPU Accelerator. Available from: https://images.nvidia.com/content/pdf/tesla/whitepaper/pascal-architecture-whitepaper.pdf [Accessed: 02-03-2018]

[23] Weber B, Tan YHM, Mahapatra S, Watson TF, Ryu H, Rahman R, et al. Spin blockade and exchange in coulomb-confined silicon double quantum dots. Nature Nanotechnology. 2014;**9**:430-435

[24] Comparing NVLink vs PCI-E with NVIDIA Tesla P100 GPUs on OpenPOWER Servers. Available from: https://www.microway.com/hpc-tech-tips/comparing-nvlink-vs-pci-e-nvidia-tesla-p100-gpus-openpower-servers/ [Accessed: 10-07-2018]

[25] Xu S, Xue W, Lin HX. Performance modeling and optimization of sparse matrix-vector multiplication on NVIDIA CUDA platform. Journal of Supercomputing. 2013;**63**:710-721. DOI: 10.1007/s11227-011-0626-0

[26] Rountree B, Ahn D, de Supinski B, Lowenthal D, Schulz M. Beyond DVFS: A first look at performance under a hardware-enforced power bound. In: Proceedings of IEEE international parallel and distributed processing symposium workshops & PHD forum (IPDPSW). 2012. pp. 947-953. DOI: 10.1109/ IPDPSW.2012.116

[27] NVIDIA management Library (NVML). Available from: https://developer. nvidia.com/nvidia-management-library-nvml [Accessed: 02-03-2018]

[28] Price of NVIDIA Tesla K40 Computing Processor GPU Cards. Available from: https://www.amazon.com/NVIDIA-Computing-Processor-Graphic-900-22081-2250-000/dp/B00KDRRTB8 [Accessed: 02-03-2018]

[29] Price of NVIDIA Tesla P100 Computing Processor GPU Cards. Available from: https://www.microway.com/hpc-tech-tips/nvidia-tesla-p100-price-analysis/ [Accessed: 02-03-2018]

Chapter 3

Characterizing Power and Energy Efficiency of Legion Data-Centric Runtime and Applications on Heterogeneous High-Performance Computing Systems

Song Huang, Song Fu, Scott Pakin and Michael Lang

Abstract

The traditional parallel programming models require programmers to explicitly specify parallelism and data movement of the underlying parallel mechanisms. Different from the traditional computation-centric programming, Legion provides a data-centric programming model for extracting parallelism and data movement. In this chapter, we aim to characterize the power and energy consumption of running HPC applications on Legion. We run benchmark applications on compute nodes equipped with both CPU and GPU, and measure the execution time, power consumption and CPU/GPU utilization. Additionally, we test the message passing interface (MPI) version of these applications and compare the performance and power consumption of high-performance computing (HPC) applications using the computation-centric and data-centric programming models. Experimental results indicate Legion applications outperforms MPI applications on both performance and energy efficiency, i.e., Legion applications can be 9.17 times as fast as MPI applications and use only 9.2% energy. Legion effectively explores the heterogeneous architecture and runs applications tasks on GPU. As far as we know, this is the first study to understand the power and energy consumption of Legion programming and runtime infrastructure. Our findings will enable HPC system designers and operators to develop and tune the performance of data-centric HPC applications with constraints on power and energy consumption.

Keywords: power consumption, Legion programming model, legion runtime, high performance computing, energy efficiency

1. Introduction

The U.S. Department of Energy (DOE) announced to invest $258 million to the exascale computing project in 2017. With funding from the six selected companies, the total investment reaches over $430 million to achieve the goal of delivering at least one exascale-capable supercomputer by 2021 [1]. Building an exascale high performance computing (HPC) system has to overcome four major challenges: parallelism, memory and storage, reliability, and energy consumption. An exascale system, if built using the existing technologies, will consume half of a gigawatt of power, which highly exceeds the expected power limit specified by DOE. Therefore, innovative technologies are needed to enhance the power and energy efficiency and improve the system performance with a low power consumption.

Compute nodes are a major power and energy consumer inside an HPC system. Deng et al. [2] found that about 60% of system power is consumed by CPU, around 30% of power is allocated to memory, and other components account for 10%. This situation becomes more obvious in HPC environments where compute intensive and data intensive computation keeps a system always busy. Hence, reducing power and energy consumption of computing units and memory is the major challenge for efficiency of the whole system.

The message passing interface (MPI) is the de facto standard for writing HPC applications. It is a computation-centric programming model, where MPI processes are independent execution units that contain instructions and state information, use their address spaces, and interact with each other via inter-process communication mechanisms defined by MPI. Application programmers focus on writing computation processes and dealing with their communication, while data-related components, including data layout, data placement, and data movement, are implicitly determined by computation. As the volume, variety, and velocity of data dramatically increase, computation-centric programming becomes inefficient. Data-centric programming is increasingly addressing these problems, because focusing on the data makes the big-data problems much simpler to express. It enables programmers to define data properties including organization, partitioning, privileges, and coherence, also allows runtime systems to control data movement, communication, task scheduling, and execution.

Legion, which is jointly developed by Stanford University, Los Alamos National laboratory, and Nvidia, is a data-centric parallel programming system for writing portable high performance programs targeted at heterogeneous architectures [3, 4]. Legion provides abstractions which allow programmers to describe properties of program data, such as independence and locality [3]. By making the Legion programming system aware of the structure of program data, it can automate many of the tedious tasks programmers currently face, including correctly extracting task- and data-level parallelism and moving data around complex memory hierarchies.

Existing works mainly focus on improving the performance of Legion applications. Little is known about the energy efficiency of the Legion system and many questions have not been answered, such as:

- Unlike the traditional HPC programming systems, what are the distinct characteristics of power and energy consumption of Legion runtime and applications?
- Can Legion applications achieve better power and energy efficiency, at the same time as accelerate the execution and increase the throughput?
- How well do Legion runtime and applications utilize computing and memory resources on both homogeneous and heterogeneous systems?

In this chapter, we study these critical questions and analyze the energy efficiency of Legion applications and runtime system. We test a number of benchmark applications with varying configurations on a CPU-GPU heterogeneous platform. We run both the MPI version and the Legion version applications. The heterogeneous system offers pure CPU and CPU-GPU execution environments. We use a variety of power profiling tools such as PAPI [5], RAPL [6], PowerAPI [7], and NVML [8] to measure runtime power consumption and characterize power consumption, energy consumption, and resource utilization of applications run on Legion. Important contributions include: (1) Legion Helper affects the performance and power consumption of applications; (2) Legion-based GPU applications perform better with regards to energy efficiency and execution time for larger problem size.

As far as we know, this is the first investigation of the performance and energy properties of Legion applications and data-centric Legion runtime system. The findings and results produced from this work will improve our understanding of Legion and develop resource scheduling to maximize system performance while operating under static/dynamic power caps.

The remainder of this chapter is structured as follows. Section 2 briefly presents the data-centric programming model and Legion runtime. The test environment (hardware, benchmarks, and profiling tools) is described in Section 3. Section 4 presents the results on performance and energy efficiency on servers with only CPU. The results on heterogeneous servers with both CPU and GPU are presented in Section 5. Key findings are highlighted in Section 6. Section 7 describes and related research and Section 8 provides the conclusion.

2. Legion programming and runtime system

Legion [3, 4] is a data-centric programming model and it provides runtime system to reduce expensive data movement in the complex memory hierarchy and to write highly portable and data intensive programs for heterogeneous system. Legion Runtime extracts independent tasks and allocates them to available computer resources to speed up parallel execution.

Compared to current computation-centric programming models, such as MPI and OpenMP, which require that programmers to explicitly specify the communication between compute nodes and data transfer for underlying parallel mechanisms, Legion focus more on defining data properties and the relationship between different data units [3]. Application developers can explicitly declare the properties of program data, including data organization, independence, partition, and locality. Therefore, Legion hides the operations of extracting parallelism and data movement and provides auto mapping to avoid suffering data moving overhead. Also, Legion allows programmers to customize optimal mapping for specific applications or infrastructure.

A dynamic scheduling approach called SOOP ("out-of-order" processor) is provided by the Legion runtime to map the dependences of tasks, distribute the tasks onto processor, map to physical instance for execution [4]. SOOP determines the task dependency at the logical region level by comparing the privileges and coherence modes to detect dependency between a newly registered task and a previous registered task. After the task dependency is satisfied, the task will be mapped and placed into the mapping queue, and scheduled to processors. Then task execution is performed and resources are recovered after execution. This whole process is automatic and hidden from Legion users. In our next discussion, we use the Legion Helper to refer to the set of processes that detect the dependency, map and dispatch of Legion tasks.

3. Evaluation environment

Before showing the experiment and discussing the results, we detail the platforms in our experimental environment in this section, provide the specifications of the homogeneous servers and heterogeneous servers, and describe the benchmark applications and profiling tools.

3.1 Hardware configurations

In the experiments, we use a homogeneous HPC server that consists of Enterprise version of Haswell processor, and a heterogeneous HPC server that has both CPU processor and a GPU accelerator. They will be referred to as the CPU server or GPU server in the following discussion.

3.1.1 CPU server

The CPU server is a Dell PowerEdge T630 computer that has two sockets with Intel Xeon E5-2683 v3 processors, 128 GB RAM and 28 TB SSD. **Table 1** contains the specification.

3.1.2 GPU server

To understand the power and energy characteristics of Legion on a heterogeneous environment, we run applications on a HP server having both Intel Xeon processor and NVIDIA Tesla K40c GPU accelerator, and another HP server with the same CPU processor and NVIDIA Tesla P100 GPU accelerator. **Table 2** shows their specifications.

3.2 Benchmark applications

To demonstrate the characteristics of the power and energy consumption of Legion runtime and application, we select two benchmark applications, which are compute-intensive, to run on both servers using Legion and MPI programming models.

3.2.1 MiniAero

MiniAero is a fluid dynamics mini-application [9, 10] designed to evaluate the programming model and hardware. It is an explicit unstructured finite volume code, which use Runge-Kutta four-order method to solve the compressible

Compute server	Dell PowerEdge T630
CPU Processor	2xIntel Xeon E5-2683 v3 (Haswell-EP)
Number of cores per socket	14
Number of threads per socket 28	28
Base frequency	2 GHz
Turbo frequency	3 GHz
Thermal design power per Socket	120 W

Table 1.
Configuration of the CPU server.

Compute server	HP ProLiant heterogeneous server
GPU processor	NVIDIA Tesla K40c
Number of CUDA cores	2880
DRAM	12 GB
Thermal design power per Socket	235w
GPU processor	NVIDIA Tesla P100
Number of CUDA cores	3584
DRAM	12 GB
Thermal design power per Socket	250w
CPU processor	Intel(R) Xeon(R) CPU X3460
Number of cores per socket	4
Number of threads per socket	8
Base frequency	2.8 GHz
Turbo frequency	3.46 GHz
Thermal design power per Socket	95 W

Table 2.
Configuration of the GPU server.

Navier-Stokes equations. It has the usual calculation and communication patterns on 3D unstructured mesh [11]. These meshes are generated on the CPU and then move to the devices (e.g. the CPU itself, GPU accelerator, or Xeon Phi). The original version of MiniAero uses multi-dimensional Kokkos arrays to store connectivity and flow data. Because MiniAero has a small dependency on tasks, the Legion version of MiniAero extracts concurrency from program data and maps it to physical regions to speed up the execution.

3.2.2 Circuit

Circuit [3] is a sample application that simulates on any graph of integrated circuit components and wires [10]. An explicit iterative solver step through time and calculates the updated voltages and currents on each node and wire. It computes the current by examining the voltage differential across every wire, updates the charge for each node with new current, and then re-calculate the voltage for every node according to the charge. The Legion runtime controls the resource allocation, performs task scheduling, and moves program data. These operations decompose independent data and allocate it to different computational units for scalability.

3.3 Profiling tools and performance metrics

3.3.1 PAPI

The Performance API (PAPI) [5] provides a set of standard APIs to access the hardware performance counter to capture real-time statistics from multiple hardware devices. The counter exist as a small set of registers, which record the occurrence of signals and events, for instance, Machine Specific Register (MSR). PAPI provides portability across different platforms via the ability to accept platform specific counter numbers. This enables the users to access a variety of devices for these counters and enable performance monitoring and tuning of these components.

3.3.2 RAPL

The Running Average Power Limit (RAPL) [6], introduced by Intel Xeon processors, which use a software power model to estimate the power and energy consumption of hardware. It can be used for monitoring of heat and energy and coverage of multiple domains such as PKG (Package Power), PP0 (Core), PP1 (uncore) and DRAM. The Haswell EP processor used in our experiments does not support PP0 and PP1 domains. Meanwhile, the RAPL counters can help to tune the performance of processors and balance the computing workloads on the nodes. In our experiments, we use the RAPL module in PAPI to profile the power consumption of the processor in the packet and DRAM domains.

3.3.3 PowerAPI

PowerAPI [7] provides a library for measuring power consumption at the process level. PowerAPI is a pure software approach to estimate power consumption of various hardware devices based on energy analytical models. Additional, the library is actor-based framework that the users can choose modules to fit for their requirements, which enables lowering computational cost and high accuracy. Moreover, PowerAPI can provide performance statistics of a particular process.

3.3.4 NVML

The NVIDIA Management Library (NVML) [8] monitors and manages NVIDIA GPU devices. It provides interfaces for querying and controlling device states, handling events, and reporting errors. Real-time query-able statistics such as ECC error counting, active processes and utilization, temperature and energy consumption can be captured via these interfaces. Also, some modifiable state can be accessed (e.g. ECC mode, compute mode, Persistence mode). In our K40c GPU and P100 GPU, we record the real-time board power draw by querying the performance counters.

4. Legion power and energy consumption on CPU server

To better understand the power and energy consumption patterns of Legion applications, we compare the performance of processors and power consumption of both MPI versions and Legion versions of *MiniAero* and the *circuit* with different problem sizes on different CPU cores.

To reduce noise and measurement errors, we perform each experiment 10 times and calculate the average of the measurements, and each run has the same initial conditions. The two applications are computationally intensive. Package and DRAM are the most important consumers of energy. To better characterize Legion applications and runtime, we separately measure and analyze the power and power consumption of Legion helper and computational processes.

4.1 Experimental results of MiniAero

For the MPI version of MiniAero, their processes have to be explicitly defined and they only share a part of the problem. The Legion version of MiniAero has some calculation processes and Legion helpers. We test the 3D-Sod with three problem sizes, that is 128 × 128 × 4, 256 × 256 × 4 and 512 × 512 × 4, on one, two and four CPU cores.

4.1.1 CPU utilization of MiniAero application

The CPU utilization, which is used to estimate the system performance, measures the percentage of CPU cycles used on a core. On a multi-core processor, a load of more than 100% indicates that two or more cores are being used by applications. **Figure 1** shows CPU usage of MiniAero with different problem sizes running on different number of CPU cores. The figures show that the CPU usage of the MPI version is relatively stable and reaches about 100%. However, for the Legion version, the CPU cycles are not fully utilized by the Legion helper when the number of compute cores is less, but the usage keep increasing as the number of cores increases. On the other hand, those CPU cycles used by computational processes are reduced in our experiments. When the core number increases from 1 to 4, shown in **Figure 1a–f** and **g–i**, the Legion helper CPU usage increases from about 48% to more than 92%. In contrast, the average CPU utilization of the calculation processes drops from 75–25%. This suggests that identifying dependencies, mapping, and scheduling tasks on Legion can cause significant overhead that interferes with the useful calculation. The problem size, however, does not affect the CPU usage very much. In **Figure 1a, d** and **g**, the execution time and CPU utilization of the Legion version are almost identical, while the execution time of the MPI version increases exponentially. Other experimental results with same number of compute cores show a similar trend. The Legion runtime system offers better scalability.

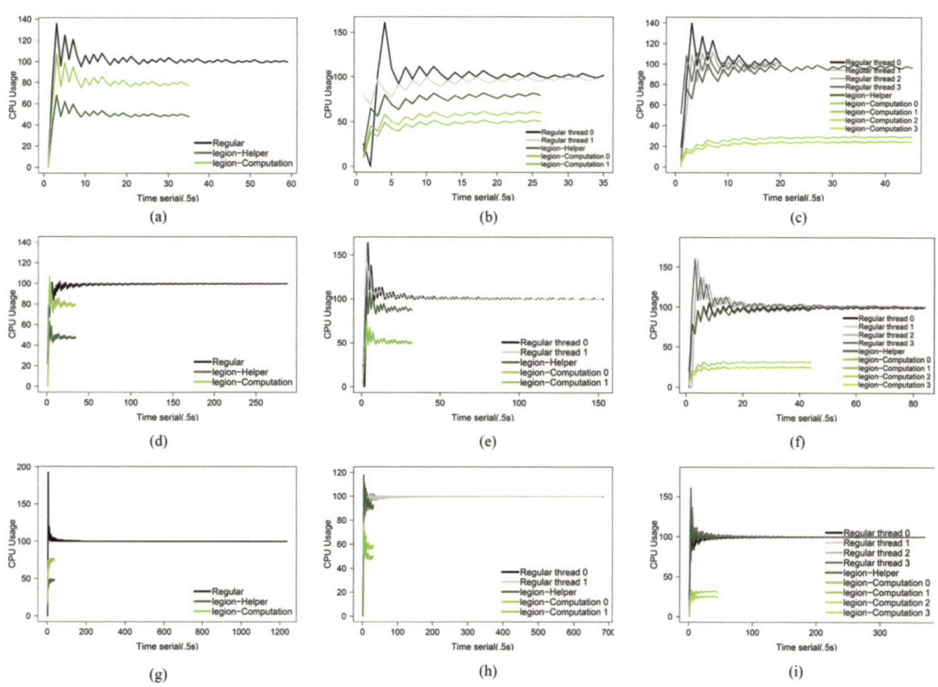

Figure 1.
*CPU utilization of MPI and Legion versions of the MiniAero application (a) Workload:128*128*4, 1 core, (b) Workload: 128*128*4, 2 cores, (c) Workload: 128*128*4, 4 cores, (d) Workload: 256*256*4, 1 core, (e) Workload: 256*256*4, 2 cores, (f) Workload: 256*256*4, 4 cores, (g) Workload: 512*512*4, 1 core, (h) Workload: 512*512*4, 2 cores, and (i) Workload: 512*512*4, 4 cores.*

4.1.2 Power usage of MiniAero application

The power consumption of the package and DRAM of both processors is similar. The biggest difference which is 12 W between packages is observed when MiniAero runs on a core as shown in **Figure 2a, d** and **g**. With the Legion runtime, the threads for arithmetic computational tasks are evenly pinned to cores of the two processors, while the Legion helper threads hovers between the cores and migrate across the cores some time. When the Legion helper floats to a processor running computational processes, the power consumption of that processor increases. For example, **Figure 2b** shows that the Legion helper is running on processor 0 and two computation processes are running on processors 0 and 1. Therefore, Package 0 draws 5.1 W more power when the processor is running at peak power. In **Figure 2c**, however, the Legion Helper runs on processor 1, which leads to more power consumption through this package. Despite this uncertainty, the total power consumption of both packages does not vary much when using the same number of cores. For example, in **Figure 2c, f** and **i**, the total power consumption of the package is 83.7–85.2 W. Memory consumes a small amount of power, that is 3.1–4.5 W and the variation is small as well. Combined with the CPU utilization results discussed in the previous subsection, we can observe that when the number of cores increases, the Legion Helper uses more CPU cycles and power consumption are also increased.

The total power consumption when running the Legion version, including both the computational tasks and the Legion helper, is 71.3–80.7% of that for the MPI version. The two limits are reached when the workload is 128 × 128 × 4. The

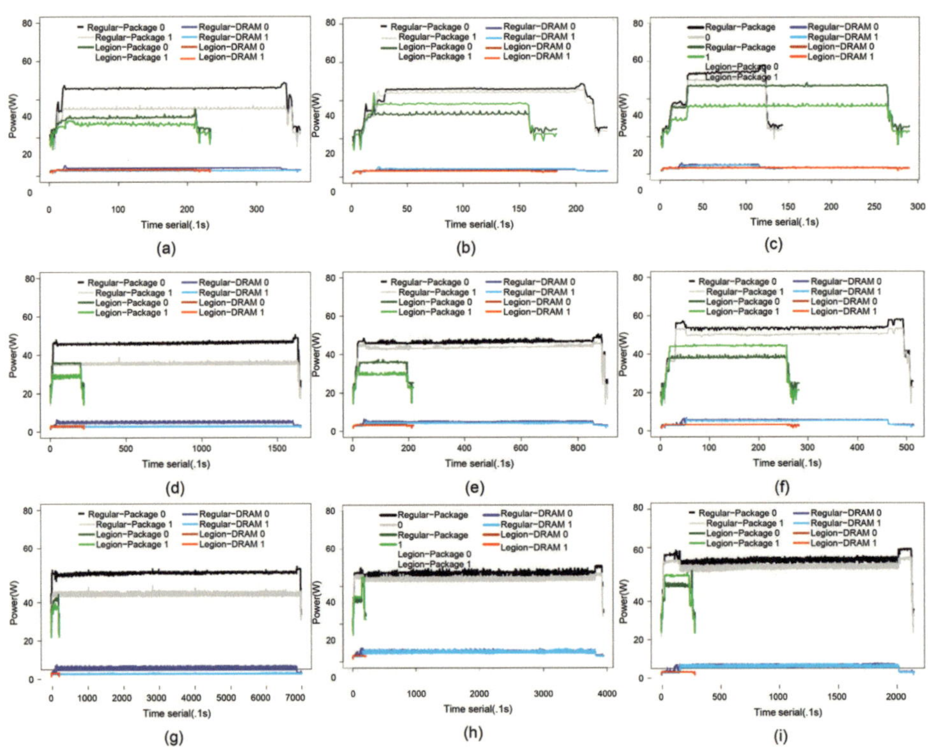

Figure 2.
*Package and DRAM power consumption of MPI and Legion versions of the MiniAero application (a) Workload: 128*128*4 1 core, (b) Workload: 128*128*4, 2 cores, (c) Workload: 128*128*4, 4 cores, (d) Workload: 256*256*4 1core, (e) Workload: 256*256*4, 2 cores, (f) Workload: 256*256*4 4 cores, (g) Workload: 512*512*4, 1 core, (h) Workload: 512*512*4, 2 cores, and (i) Workload: 512*512*4, 4 cores.*

power consumption of the Legion version on 1, 2 and 4 cores is 57.8, 72.6 and 81.7 W respectively, while the MPI counterpart consumes 81.1, 90 and 101.2 W.

In addition, we use PowerAPI to measure the power consumption of the MPI version and Legion version of MiniAero at the process level. The power consumption is depicted in **Figure 3**. **Figure 3** compares the power consumption of processors measured by *PowerAPI* on varying problem sizes and settings (128 × 128 × 4, 256 × 256 × 4, 512 × 512 × 4 on 1,2,4 cores respectively). The power consumption measured by PowerAPI is close to the results provided by RAPL. Overall, the difference between the two tools is within a range of [2.4w, 2.9w]. As both versions of MiniAero consume a little amount of power from DRAM, we do not include it in the figure.

4.1.3 Execution time and energy consumption of MiniAero

The execution time as shown in **Figure 4** and energy consumption as shown in **Figure 5** of Legion-version of MiniAero are relatively stable except the rise, when the Legion helper sends tasks to more cores for parallelism. In contrast, the MPI version follows the normal trend, where more cores accelerate execution and save energy. The results indicate that while Legion provides more partitions for the application, it distributes the workload equally among the cores and slows down tasks, which can be caused by the Legion helper. As a result, the power consumption of each processor does not change much while the execution time is prolonged, resulting in increased power consumption. The MPI version, on the other hand, fully exploits the extra cores, reducing execution time and power consumption.

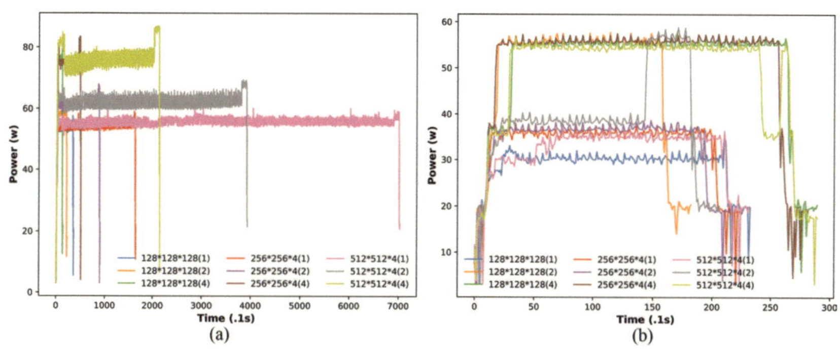

Figure 3.
Power consumption of MPI version of MiniAero measured by Power API (a) Power consumption of MPI version of MiniAero mea- sured by Power API, and (b) Power consumption of Legion version of MiniAero measured by Power API.

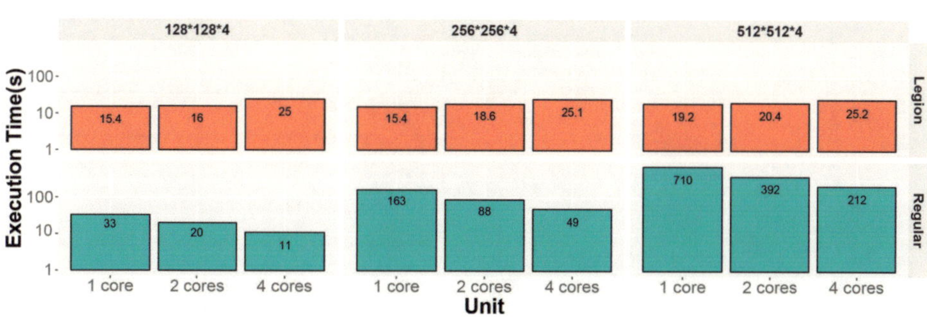

Figure 4.
Execution time of the MiniAero application.

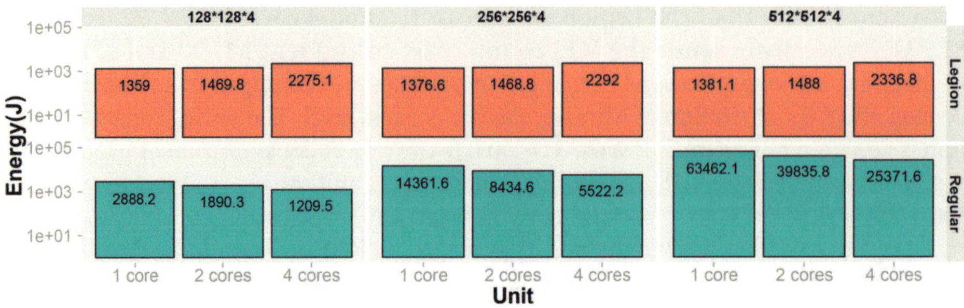

Figure 5.
Energy consumption of the MiniAero application.

The highest reduction in Legion execution time and energy is achieved when using a single core for a 512 × 512 × 4 problem size. The MPI version requires 36 times more execution time, and 45 times more energy than the Legion version respectively. Although the Legion helper causes more overhead, it reduces 89.1% of execution time and saves 90.8% energy compared to its MPI counterpart.

4.2 Experimental results of circuit

The Legion version of the circuit application is much more scalable than Legion version of MiniAero. The CPU utilization of Legion Helper jump to 17% at the beginning of the execution, and then the amount of utilization drops to 5% for the rest of the execution, as shown in **Figure 6a**. On the other hand, the CPU cores that perform computational tasks are fully used and the utilization is over 100% sometime. All the execution of *Circuit* on different numbers of cores has similar pattern.

In **Figure 6b** display that more power is consumed by the packet domain when more cores are used for computational tasks. From one core to two cores, power consumption increases by 6.6 W and an additional 6.8 W is consumed by two cores into four cores. In the meanwhile, the power draw of DRAM remains low and constant.

It is also shown in **Figure 7** that with more cores for computational tasks, execution time and power consumption are reduced. For example, if you run on two cores and four cores, 49.7 and 73.3% of execution time and 42.3 and 64.1% of energy, respectively, is reduced as if only one core is running.

The power per watt of the Legion version of the circuit is 6.7 MFLOPS/W on a core. It reaches 11.6 MFLOPS/W on two cores and 18.0 MFLOPS/W on 4 cores,

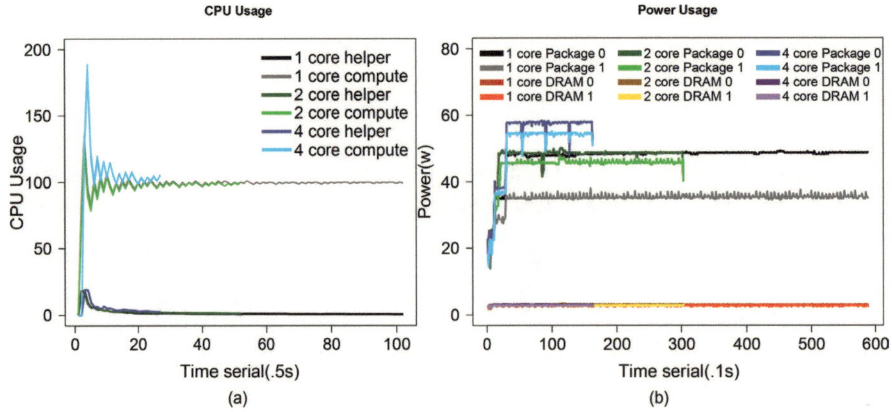

Figure 6.
CPU utilization and power consumption of the circuit application (a) CPU utilization, and (b) Power consumption.

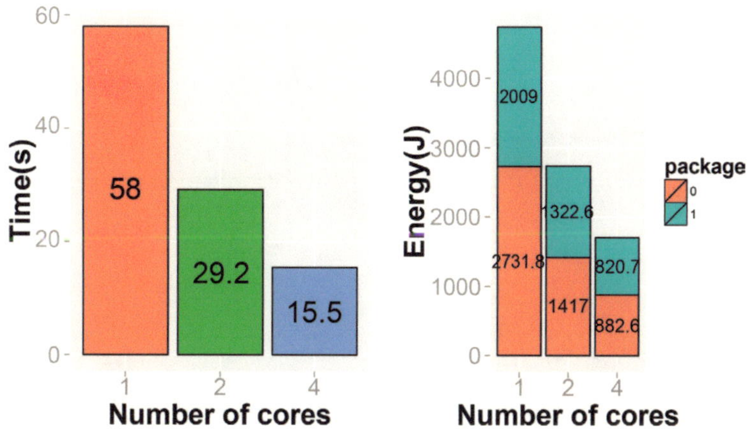

Figure 7.
Execution time and energy consumption of the circuit application.

which is 1.73 times and 1.55 times higher than one core and two cores. This observation indicates good scalability and energy efficiency of Legion runtime and application.

5. Power and energy consumption with legion on CPU-GPU server

To discover the power and energy consumption of Legion runtime and application on heterogeneous platform, we perform *circuit* tasks on GPU cores and compare them to the results of the CPU server. The Legion helper of the circuit identifies dependencies, maps logical areas, schedules tasks on CPU cores, and performs tasks on GPU CUDA cores.

5.1 CPU utilization of circuit

Figure 8 shows the resource usage when connecting to the CPU server and the heterogeneous server. During the initialization phase, the CPU utilization on both platforms has a steep jump and reach beyond 100%, while the GPU utilization remain 0. After that, the GPU starts with parallel circuit tasks. For the two problem sizes (2 loops and 4 pieces, 4 loops and 8 pieces) shown in **Figure 8**, the circuit tasks run at a high CPU utilization of nearly 100%. The *Circuit* takes advantage of 2880 CUDA cores in the Tesla K40c GPU, and the massive parallelism leads to a distinct reduced execution time. In **Figure 8a**, the execution time of the circuit on the GPU server is only about 1/3 of that on the CPU server, although the initialization phase requires another 7.6 s. The larger problem size, as shown in **Figure 8b**, causes the execution time on the CPU server to be increased 3.2-fold, while the increase on the GPU is only 0.8-fold. This indicates that Legion scales are scaled very well in the heterogeneous CPU-GPU environment.

5.2 Power consumption of circuit on heterogeneous server

Figure 9 shows the power consumption of the circuit on the CPU server and heterogeneous server with Tesla K40c. The power consumption of the CPU at the process level, measured with PowerAPI [7], is 3.05 W and remains stable in both cases. The power consumption of GPU, as measured by NVML [8], varies as the problem size changes; which is 50.5 W for 2 loops and 4 pieces of components and 55.1 W for 4 loops and 8 pieces of components respectively. This is because GPU

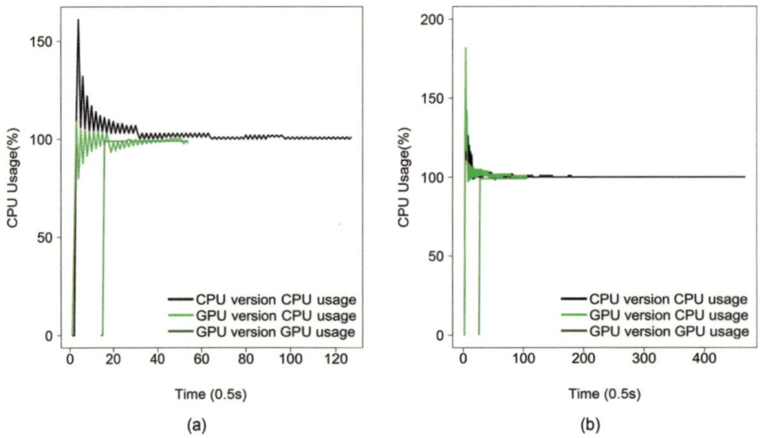

Figure 8.
The circuit application run on CPU-GPU heterogeneous server (a) CPU utilization of circuit (loops = 2 and pieces= 4), and (b) CPU utilization of circuit (loops = 4 and pieces= 8).

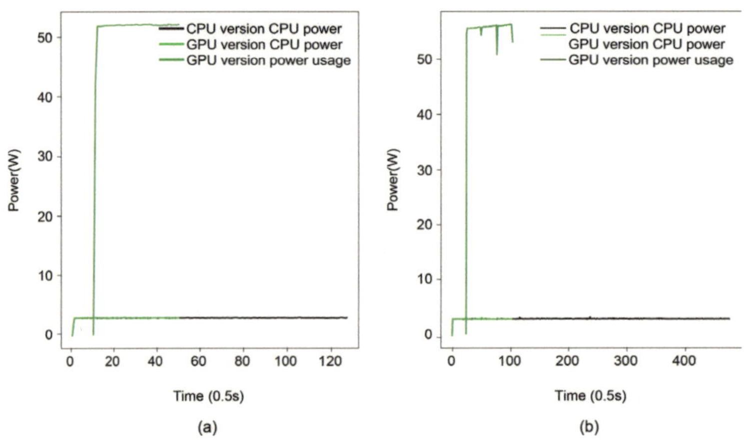

Figure 9.
Power consumption of circuit on the heterogeneous server. The CPU power usage is measured by PowerAPI, and the GPU power usage is measured by NVML (a) Power consumption of circuit (loops = 2 and pieces = 4), and (b) Power consumption of circuit (loops = 4 and pieces = 8).

has more capacity to handle more independent tasks and gain more throughput but consume more power.

5.3 Execution time and energy consumption of *Circuit*

Figure 10 depicts the execution time and energy consumption of the *Circuit*. Not surprisingly, the GPU version of *Circuit* runs on heterogeneous platform shorten the execution time but at the cost of consuming more power. For the problem size of 2 Loops and 4 Pieces, it takes 65.3 s for CPU version and 26.7 s for GPU version to execute, and consumes 389.6 J and 2164.1 J energy respectively. That means CPU version takes 1.45 times more execution time and saves 72.0% of the power compared to the GPU execution. In another situation for the problem size of 4 Loops and 8 Pieces, it takes 240.4 s and 1469.9 J for CPU version, and 53.9 s and 4782.6 J for GPU version to execute. That means CPU version of the circuit takes 3.46 times more execution time and saves 69.3% of the energy. This result indicates that Legion applications with large problem sizes should be delivered onto heterogeneous platform to reduce their execution time, which can lead to a slight increase in energy consumption.

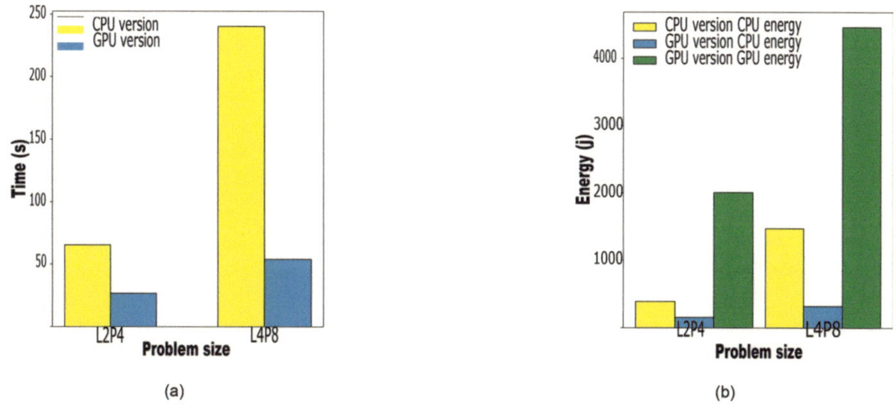

Figure 10.
Execution time and energy consumption of circuit on two platforms (a) Execution time of circuit, and (b) Energy consumption of circuit.

5.4 Influence of GPU frequency scaling

Dynamic voltage and frequency scaling (DVFS) is often used to find the best configuration for optimal energy and energy savings. **Figure 12** compares the performance of circuit running on GPU accelerator with different frequencies scaling, where **Figure 11** shows the power consumption of circuit running on different frequencies, **Figure 12a** compares the execution time. **Figure 12b** and **c** describe the energy consumption and the "FLOPS" which indicate the energy efficiency of the circuit application. From the figure we can see that the standard frequency which is 745 MHz of the Tesla K40c GPU is not the best setting for the Legion circuit. With the lowest frequency at 324 MHz, the circuit takes 2.21 times more execution time

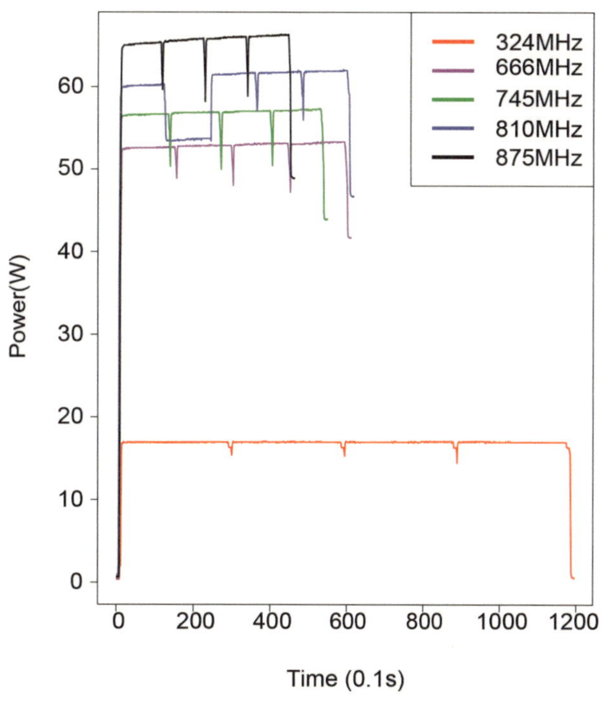

Figure 11.
Power consumption with GPU frequency scaling.

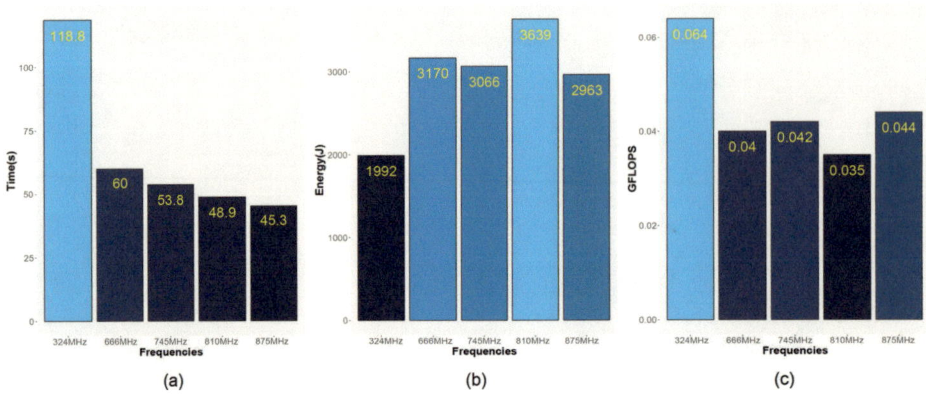

Figure 12.
Performance of circuit run at different GPU frequencies (loops = 4 and pieces = 8) (a) Execution time of different GPU frequency scaling, (b) Energy Consumption of different frequency GPU scaling, and (c) FLOPS of different frequency GPU scaling.

while saving 35% of power. Execution time is reduced by 18.8 with 3.4% energy savings when operating the circuit with the highest GPU frequency. In both cases the power consumption is lower than at the standard frequency. Both frequency settings provide good energy efficiency. The frequency selection depends on the power requirements.

To follow the advance of hardware technology, we not only test Legion applications on our Nvidia K40 GPU, but also run the Legion version of circuit on a new GPU, that is P100 GPU Accelerator(12 GB Card). We scale the frequency of P100 to its base frequency at 1126 MHz and its max frequency at 1303 MHz to evaluate the performance of circuit. **Figure 13** shows the performance of the Legion version of circuit with a workload of loops = 4 and pieces = 8. From **Figure 13a**, we can see if the frequency of P100 is set to 1303 MHz, the power consumption exceeds 100 W, while the power consumption is around 88 W, if the frequency is set to 1126 MHz. **Figure 13b–d** depict the execution time, energy consumption, and the processing power of P100 for Legion circuit respectively. Compared to Tesla K40c, there is a big improvement on performance, while the energy consumption has a significant drop. This is due to the reduced execution

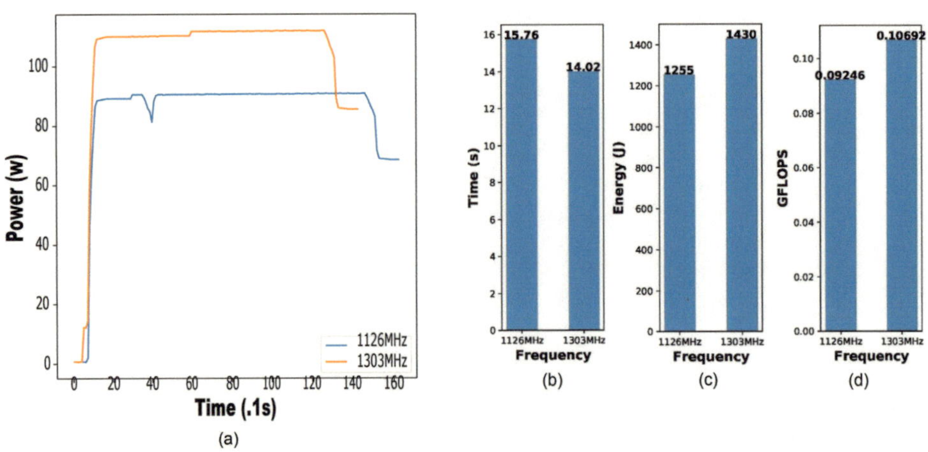

Figure 13.
Performance of circuit run at different GPU frequencies (loops = 4 and pieces = 8) (a) Power consumption of different GPU frequency scaling, (b) Execution time, (c) Energy, and (d) GFLOPS.

time. Hence, we expect that the Legion version of circuit will have a better performance on the latest GPUs.

6. Findings and discussion

The Legion -based MiniAero is a good example to highlight the Legion Helper's scalability problem. If the Legion helper is unable to isolate independent tasks quickly enough with the increased number of associated compute resources (such as CPU cores), this becomes a performance bottleneck. The resource utilization of Legion helper processes continues to increase and the throughput of compute tasks decreases. This leads to a longer execution time and reduced energy efficiency.

In cases where the Legion system and legacy applications have good scalability, energy and energy savings become more effective as more computational resources are used. The execution time of an application is significantly reduced, while the power consumption does not increase much, resulting in better energy efficiency.

Legion offers significant benefits through GPU computing. As GPU-mapped and scheduled tasks can be performed in parallel, performance enhancement and energy efficiency can be further improved.

7. Related works

Some new Legion program model features, model components, and how these components work were presented in [4]. A combination of static and dynamic checks to improve the solidity of the Legion system and a compositional parallel semantics are described in [12]. An event-based runtime system [13] is embedded in Legion asynchronously for heterogeneous and distributed storage architectures. Structure slicing [14] breaks the specification of data usage, identifies data parallelism, and reduces data movement. A highly productive programming language, Regent [10], which can be translated into Legion implementation, runs sequentially without explicit synchronization.

Power profiling in production computer systems provides valuable data and knowledge for the development of power simulators and resource scheduling policies. Fine-grained power profiling techniques measure the power consumption of individual hardware components such as CPU [15], memory [16], hard disk [17] and other devices [18]. In contrast, coarse-grained performance profiling aims to characterize system-wide performance dynamics, such as the macro stream framework [19]. Moreover, a power meter for virtualized environments was presented in [20]. CPU event counters and the Performance Programming Interface Library were used to estimate the power usage on a per-thread basis. Kamil et al. profiled HPC applications on multiple test platforms and projected the performance profiling results from a single node to a complete system [21]. Ge et al. investigated the influence of software and hardware configurations on system-wide power consumption [22]. They found that properties of HPC applications affect the power consumption of a system. Hackenberg et al. conducted a detailed analysis of Haswell's P-state and C-state transition latencies and the impact of Haswell's new power management mechanisms on memory bandwidth and performance reproducibility [23]. Our work differs from these previous efforts by measuring and analyzing the impact of new Haswell power management capabilities on the performance and performance of HPC codes.

Some researchers analyzed the power and energy efficiency of different types of applications run on HPC systems. Bari et al. investigated OpenMP's runtime configurations on power constrained systems at different power levels [24]. They found that a suitable selection of OpenMP's runtime parameters could improve the execution time and reduce the energy consumption of a parallel program by up to 67 and 72%, respectively. Qasem et al. [25] evaluated the impact of data layout and placement on the energy efficiency of heterogeneous applications by means of memory divergence, data access patterns, arithmetic intensities and data placement. They found that data layout and placement had a significant impact on the energy efficiency. Additionally, analytical models were developed to analyze energy efficiency in [26]. The models were able to support a priori selection of the operating frequency that leaded to a near optimal energy consumption for the execution of multi-threading applications. Meanwhile, Heinrich et al. aimed to predict the energy consumption of MPI applications by developing a computation model, a communication model, and an energy model which were integrated into the SimGrid simulation toolkit [27]. To improve the system performance by utilizing the available power budget more efficiently on multiple-node platforms, a hierarchical multi-dimensional power aware allocation framework was developed in [28] for power bounded parallel computing. The power allocation was performed using memory power-level settings, thread concurrency throttling, and core-thread affinity, and the scheduler outperformed other methods by 20% on average.

To control the power consumption of HPC systems, power limitation [29] is a promising and effective approach. System operators can balance the performance and power consumption of clusters by adjusting the maximum amount of power (also called the power budget) that clusters can consume. Pelly et al. presented a dynamic current sourcing and coverage method at the [30] Power Distribution Unit (PDU). They proposed using a heuristic policy to shift the capacity weakness to servers with increasing power requirements. Zhang et al. proposed a hybrid software/hardware power capping system and proved that their power cap outperforms the hardware power capping system provided by Intel and has the same reaction time [31]. For HPC jobs, many factors affect power consumption, including hardware configurations and resource usage. Femal et al. developed a hierarchical management policy to distribute the power budget to clusters [32]. Kim et al. investigated the relationship between CPU voltages and system performance and energy efficiency [33]. Utilizing Dynamic Voltage Scaling (DVS) technologies, a Task Planning Policy has been proposed that aims to minimize energy consumption while meeting specified performance requirements. Rountree et al. proposed guidelines for overprovisioning hardware with hardware-enforced performance limitations and system-wide performance reallocation in an application-independent manner [34, 35]. We have developed a complete system simulator, TracSim [36], which estimates the capacity of trapped energy under various power-limiting and job-planning guidelines.

8. Conclusion

In this chapter, we describe the power consumption, energy efficiency, performance, and resource usage of Legion runtime environment and applications. Our experimental results show that Legion offers favorable energy efficiency, although in some cases its scalability can be influenced by Legion Helpers. The Legion programming model is consistent with the massively parallel nature of the GPU design and shows good performance and energy efficiency for large problem-size applications.

Acknowledgements

This work is supported by the U.S. Department of Energy contract DE-AC52-06NA25396. This chapter has been assigned the LANL identifier LA-UR-16-25965.

Conflict of interest

The authors declare no conflict of interest.

Author details

Song Huang[1], Song Fu[1*], Scott Pakin[2] and Michael Lang[2]

1 University of North Texas, Denton, Texas, USA

2 Los Alamos National Laboratory, Los Alamos, New Mexico, USA

*Address all correspondence to: song.fu@unt.edu

References

[1] D. of Energy. Department of Energy Awards Six Research Contracts Totaling $258 million to Accelerate U.S. Supercomputing Technology; 2017

[2] Deng Q, Meisner D, Bhattacharjee A, Wenisch TF, Bianchini R. Coscale: Coordinating cpu and memory system dvfs in server systems. In: Proceedings of the 2012 45th Annual IEEE/ACM International Symposium on Microarchitecture. IEEE Computer Society; 2012. pp. 143-154

[3] Legion Project. http://legion.stanford.edu/. 2016

[4] Bauer M, Treichler S, Slaughter E, Aiken A. Legion: Expressing locality and independence with logical regions. In: High Performance Computing, Networking, Storage and Analysis (SC), 2012 International Conference for. IEEE; 2012. pp. 1-11

[5] Mucci PJ, Browne S, Deane C, Ho G. Papi: A portable interface to hardware performance counters. In: Proceedings of the Department of Defense HPCMP users Group Conference. Vol. 710. 1999

[6] David H, Gorbatov E, Hanebutte UR, Khanna R, Le C. Rapl: Memory power estimation and capping. In: Proceedings of the 16th ACM/IEEE International Symposium on Low Power Electronics and Design. ACM; 2010. pp. 189-194

[7] Bourdon A, Noureddine A, Rouvoy R, Seinturier L. PowerAPI: A software library to monitor the energy consumed at the process-level. ERCIM News. 2013;**92**:2013

[8] NVIDIA. Nvidia management library (nvml), 2016

[9] Mantevo Project. https://mantevo.org/packages/. 2016

[10] Slaughter E, Lee W, Treichler S, Bauer M, Aiken A. Regent: A high-productivity programming language for hpc with logical regions. In: Proceedings of the International Conference for High Performance Computing, Networking, Storage and Analysis. ACM; 2015. p. 81

[11] Hollman DS, Hollman DS, et al. Lessons Learned from Porting the Miniaero Application to Charm++. Technical report. Sandia National Laboratories; 2015

[12] Treichler S, Bauer M, Aiken A. Language support for dynamic, hierarchical data partitioning. In: ACM SIGPLAN Notices. Vol. 48. ACM; 2013. pp. 495-514

[13] Aiken A, Bauer M, Treichler S. Realm: An event-based low-level runtime for distributed memory architectures. In: Parallel Architecture and Compilation Techniques (PACT), 2014 23rd International Conference on. IEEE; 2014. pp. 263-275

[14] Bauer M, Treichler S, Slaughter E, Aiken A. Structure slicing: Extending logical regions with fields. In: Proceedings of the International Conference for High Performance Computing, Networking, Storage and Analysis. IEEE Press; 2014. pp. 845-856

[15] Magklis G, Scott ML, Semeraro G, Albonesi DH, Dropsho S. Profile-based dynamic voltage and frequency scaling for a multiple clock domain microprocessor. ACM SIGARCH Computer Architecture News. 2003;**31**(2):14-27

[16] Ye W, Vijaykrishnan N, Kandemir M, Irwin MJ. The design and use of simplepower: A cycle-accurate energy estimation tool. In: Proceedings of the 37th Annual Design Automation Conference. ACM; 2000. pp. 340-345

[17] Zedlewski J, Sobti S, Garg N, Zheng F, Krishnamurthy A, Wang RY, et al. Modeling hard-disk power consumption. In: FAST. Vol. 3. 2003. pp. 217-230

[18] Ye TT, Benini L, De Micheli G. Analysis of power consumption on switch fabrics in network routers. In: Design Automation Conference, 2002. Proceedings. 39th. IEEE; 2002. pp. 524-529

[19] Zhang Z, Fu S. Macropower: A coarse-grain power profiling framework for energy-efficient cloud computing. In: Performance Computing and Communications Conference (IPCCC), 2011 IEEE 30th International. IEEE; 2011. pp. 1-8

[20] Phung J, Lee YC, Zomaya AY. Application-agnostic power monitoring in virtualized environments. In: Cluster, Cloud and Grid Computing (CCGRID), 2017 17th IEEE/ACM International Symposium on. IEEE; 2017. pp. 335-344

[21] Kamil S, Shalf J, Strohmaier E. Power efficiency in high performance computing. In: Parallel and Distributed Processing, 2008. IPDPS 2008. IEEE International Symposium on. IEEE; 2008. pp. 1-8

[22] Ge R, Feng X, Song S, Chang H-C, Li D, Cameron KW. Powerpack: Energy profiling and analysis of high-performance systems and applications. IEEE Transactions on Parallel and Distributed Systems. 2010;**21**(5):658-671

[23] Hackenberg D, Schöne R, Ilsche T, Molka D, Schuchart J, Geyer R. An energy efficiency feature survey of the intel Haswell processor. In: Parallel and Distributed Processing Symposium Workshop (IPDPSW), 2015 IEEE International. IEEE; 2015. pp. 896-904

[24] Bari MAS, Malik AM, Qawasmeh A, Chapman B. A detailed analysis of OpenMP runtime configurations for power constrained systems. In: 2017 Eighth International Green and Sustainable Computing Conference (IGSC). IEEE; 2017. pp. 1-8

[25] Qasem A, Teich S. Evaluating the impact of data layout and placement on the energy efficiency of heterogeneous applications. In: Green and Sustainable Computing Conference (IGSC), 2017 Eighth International. IEEE; 2017. pp. 1-8

[26] Rauber T, Runger G, Stachowski M. Model-based optimization of the energy efficiency of multi-threaded applications. In: 2017 Eighth International Green and Sustainable Computing Conference (IGSC). IEEE; 2017. pp. 1-6

[27] Heinrich FC, Cornebize T, Degomme A, Legrand A, Carpen-Amarie A, Hunold S, et al. Predicting the energy-consumption of mpi applications at scale using only a single node. In: Cluster Computing (CLUSTER), 2017 IEEE International Conference on. IEEE; 2017. pp. 92-102

[28] Zou P, Allen T, Davis CH IV, Feng X, Ge R. Clip: Cluster-level intelligent power coordination for power-bounded systems. In: Cluster Computing (CLUSTER), 2017 IEEE International Conference on. IEEE; 2017. pp. 541-551

[29] Choi J, Govindan S, Urgaonkar B, Sivasubramaniam A. Profiling, prediction, and capping of power consumption in consolidated environments. In: Modeling, Analysis and Simulation of Computers and Telecommunication Systems, 2008. MASCOTS 2008. IEEE International Symposium on. IEEE; 2008. pp. 1-10

[30] Pelley S, Meisner D, Zandevakili P, Wenisch TF, Underwood J. Power routing: Dynamic power provisioning

in the data center. In: ACM Sigplan Notices. Vol. 45. 2010. pp. 231-242

[31] Zhang H, Hoffmann H. Maximizing performance under a power cap: A comparison of hardware, software, and hybrid techniques. ACM SIGARCH Computer Architecture News. 2016;**44**(2):545-559

[32] Femal ME, Freeh VW. Boosting data center performance through non-uniform power allocation. In: Autonomic Computing, 2005. ICAC 2005. Proceedings. Second International Conference on. IEEE; 2005. pp. 250-261

[33] Kim KH, Buyya R, Kim J. Power aware scheduling of bag-of-tasks applications with deadline constraints on Dvs-enabled clusters. In: CCGrid; 2007

[34] Ellsworth DA, Malony AD, Rountree B, Schulz M. POW: System-wide dynamic reallocation of limited power in HPC. In: Proc. of HPDC. 2015

[35] Patki T, Lowenthal DK, Rountree B, Schulz M, De Supinski BR. Exploring hardware overprovisioning in power-constrained, high performance computing. In: Proceedings of the 27th international ACM conference on International conference on supercomputing. ACM; 2013. pp. 173-182

[36] Zhang Z, Lang M, Pakin S, Fu S. Trapped capacity: Scheduling under a power cap to maximize machine-room throughput. In: Proceedings of the 2nd International Workshop on Energy Efficient Supercomputing. IEEE Press; 2014. pp. 41-50

Chapter 4

Security Applications of GPUs

Giorgos Vasiliadis

Abstract

Despite the recent advances in software security hardening techniques, vulnerabilities can always be exploited if the attackers are really determined. Regardless the protection enabled, successful exploitation can always be achieved, even though admittedly, today, it is much harder than it was in the past. Since securing software is still under ongoing research, the community investigates detection methods in order to protect software. Three of the most promising such methods are monitoring the (i) network, (ii) the filesystem, and (iii) the host memory, for possible exploitation. Whenever a malicious operation is detected then the monitor should be able to terminate it and/or alert the administrator. In this chapter, we explore how to utilize the highly parallel capabilities of modern commodity graphics processing units (GPUs) in order to improve the performance of different security tools operating at the network, storage, and memory level, and how they can offload the CPU whenever possible. Our results show that modern GPUs can be very efficient and highly effective at accelerating the pattern matching operations of network intrusion detection systems and antivirus tools, as well as for monitoring the integrity of the base computing systems.

Keywords: security, network security, host security, intrusion detection, antivirus, kernel integrity monitoring

1. Introduction

The ever-increasing amount of malicious software (malware) constitutes an enormous challenge to network operators, IT administrators, as well as ordinary home users. To protect against such an evolving threat landscape, it is necessary to provide detection of malicious activities at different levels: (i) by inspected exchanged data at central network traffic ingress points, (ii) by scanning of unwanted software at the storage level, and (iii) by providing program memory integrity at the host level. Three of the most widely used tools that perform such kind of operations are intrusion detection systems, antivirus software, and host integrity tools. Unfortunately, the constant increase in link speeds, storage capacity, number of end-devices and the sheer number of malware, poses significant challenges to all these tools, which end up requiring high scanning throughput and low latency.

Typically, the detection of malicious activities spends the majority of its time matching data streams against a large set of known signatures or checksums, using string searching, regular expression matching and hashing algorithms. Signature matching algorithms analyze the data stream and compare it against a database of fixed strings or regular expressions to detect known malware. The signature patterns can be quite complex, composed of wild-card characters, range constraints, different-size strings, and sometimes recursive forms. To make matters worse, the number of signatures is increasing proportional every year, as the amount of malware grows, exposing scaling problems of anti-malware products.

Modern GPUs have been proven to be highly effective and very efficient at accelerating computational- and memory-intensive workloads. The ever-growing video game industry is a driving factor for becoming ever more powerful and flexible stream processors, specialized for highly parallel operations. Comparing with commodity CPUs, the massive number of transistors is devoted to data processing, rather than data caching and flow control, making them ideal to perform data parallel computations that up till now were handled by the CPU.

In this chapter, we present new models for malware detection tools that operate at the network, storage, and memory level. These models combine the commodity, general-purpose GPU paradigms, tailored for high-performance and low-latency analysis. Our systems take advantage of the parallelism offered by the GPUs to improve scalability and runtime performance and are able to offload the CPU whenever possible. Our results show that modern GPUs can be highly effective and very efficient at accelerating a highly diverse set of operations that are core functions of modern security tools, including string searching, regular expression matching and checksum computations.

2. Network intrusion detection and prevention systems

First, we show how to exploit the parallelism of the graphics processing unit (GPU) to offload specific intensive tasks of a network intrusion detection system (NIDS). Particularly, we present the design, implementation, and evaluation of string searching and regular expression algorithms engines running on GPUs. We have integrated these implementations in the popular Snort intrusion detection system [1] to offload both string and regular expression matching computation, as shown in **Figure 1**.

The data parallel capabilities of modern GPUs can allow the concurrent matching of multiple input data streams at the same time against a large set of fixed string patterns and regular expressions. Mainly, the architecture can be separated in several different tasks: packet capturing, decoding, preprocesing, the transfer of the network packets to the GPU, the string-matching on the GPU, and the transfer of the matching results back to the CPU, where all the remaining conditions of the detection rules are checked. Whenever a packet needs to be scanned against a regular expression, it is subsequently transferred back to the GPU where the actual matching takes place.

2.1 Architecture

The overall design of our GPU-assisted network intrusion detection architecture, has two key factors for achieving good performance: (i) load balancing between processing units, and (ii) linear performance scalability with the addition of more processing units. In particular, the monitored traffic is distributed at the flow-level to different CPU cores, by applying a symmetric hash function on the 5-tuple fields of each packet header (i.e., source IP address, destination IP address, source port, destination port, protocol). Eventually, all packets of the same flow (i.e., same connection) will always be placed in the same ring buffer, and will be processed by the same CPU-core. This inherently leads us to a multicore architecture, in which each core processes an evenly distributed portion of

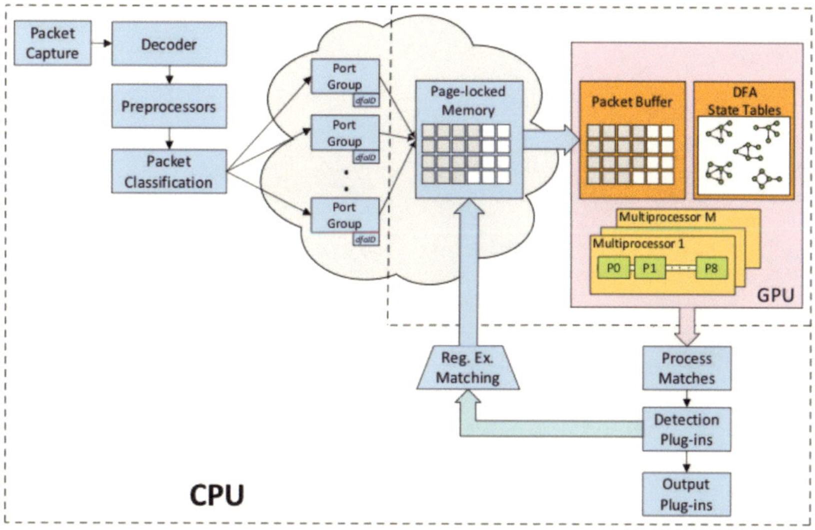

Figure 1.
Overview of the single-threaded GPU-based network intrusion detection architecture.

the network traffic, without requiring any intra-node communication for processing operations that are limited in scope to a single flow. Each CPU core is responsible for network flow tracking, protocol parsing, TCP stream reassembly, and content normalization. The reassembled and normalized packets of each network flow are then transferred to the graphics card in large batches, in order to be processed in parallel. This enables an "intra-flow" parallelism, in which network packets from the same flow can be processed in parallel, while also maintaining flow-state dependencies. We note that this buffering scheme, as well as the extra data transfer operations that need to be performed between the memory address spaces of each device obviously, adds some latency to the processing path. Even though the computational gains offered by the GPU tolerates these extra data transfers and pay off in terms of increased throughput, we further mitigate these overheads by implementing pipelining schemes that allow the CPU and GPU execution to overlap, thus offering an additional level of parallelism to the overall execution path (see Section 2.1.3). Overall, by parallelizing both packet preprocessing and content inspection across multiple CPUs and GPUs, our proposed architecture can operate in multi-Gigabit networks using solely commodity components.

As shown in **Figure 2**, we utilize the different processing units available (i.e., CPUs and GPUs) in order to map the different functionalities that are performed across the incoming network flows, using both *task* and *data* parallelism. More specifically, the network interface distributes the incoming network packets to the CPU-cores, by applying a symmetric hash function on the 5-tuple fields of each packet header (i.e., source IP address, destination IP address, source port, destination port, protocol). This ensures that all packets of the same flow (i.e., same connection) will always be placed in the same ring buffer, and will be processed by the same CPU-core. Each CPU-core reassembles and normalizes the captured traffic before offloading it to the GPU for pattern matching [2]. Any matching results are logged by the corresponding CPU-core using the specified logging mechanism, such as a file or database.

This design has many advantages: *First*, no synchronization or lock mechanisms is needed, since different network flows will be processed by different CPU-cores independently. *Second*, each CPU-core maintains smaller data

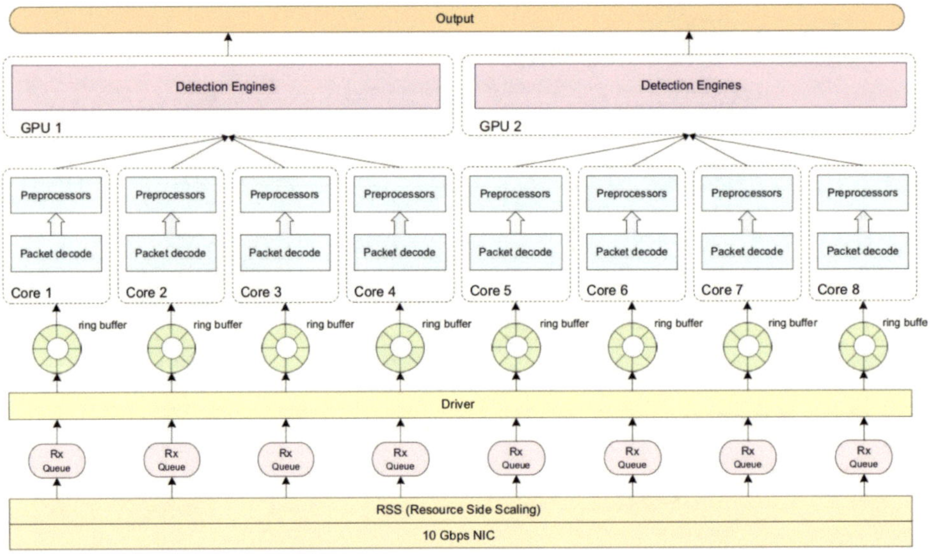

Figure 2.
The architecture of the GPU-enabled network intrusion detection system.

structures (e.g., the flow management table, the TCP reassembly tables, etc.) instead of sharing a few large ones, which reduces both the number of tables look-ups, as well as the size of the working set in each cache, increasing overall cache efficiency.

2.1.1 Parallel multi-pattern engine

A major design criterion for scanning large network data flows against many different fixed string patterns, is the choice of an efficient matching algorithm. The majority of network intrusion detection systems utilize a flavor of the Aho-Corasick algorithm [3] for string searching. Internally, the algorithm uses a transition function that computes the next state T [state, c] for a given state and a character c. A pattern is matched every time the algorithm transits to a final state. The performance and memory requirements of Aho-Corasick depend on how the transition function is implemented. In the full implementation, hereinafter AC-Full, each transition is represented with 256 elements, one for each 8-bit character. Each element contains the next state to move to, as a result the next state can be found in $O(1)$ steps for every input character; this ensures a linear complexity over the input data, independently on the number of patterns, which is very efficient in terms of performance.

However, a disadvantage of the full state representation is the large memory requirements, even for small signature sets. For Snort, the compiled state table can reach up to several hundred Megabytes of memory. To make matters worse, CPU processes cannot share memory on the GPU device, as such a different memory space has to be allocated in the GPU. This can result to significant memory allocations, as shown in **Table 1**. Given that the GeForce GTX780 that we used for our evaluation comes with 2GB of memory, only two Snort instances can fully utilize the GPU at a time.

To preserve scalability with respect to the number of concurrently running Snort instances, it is important to optimize the memory requirements needed. As such, instead of using the full state table representation, we use a compacted version, similar to [4], in which the states are represented in a banded-row format. In particular, we store only the elements from the first non-zero value to the last

#Rules	#Patterns	#States	AC-Full	AC-Compact
8192	193,167	1,703,023	890.46 MB	24.18 MB

Table 1.
Memory requirements of AC-Full and AC-Compact for the default Snort rule set.

non-zero value of the table; the number of the stored elements is known as the bandwidth of the sparse table. Obviously, in the compacted implementation, namely AC-Compact, the next state cannot be accessed directly while matching input bytes. Instead, it has to be computed, as shown in **Figure 3**; this computation obviously adds a small overhead at the scanning phase, which is amortized though by the significantly lower memory consumption.

Moreover, it is common that some patterns may share the same final state in the state table or be case-insensitive. Instead of adding every different combination of capital and lower letters for every case-insensitive pattern, we simply mark that pattern as case-insensitive and add only one combination (i.e., all characters are converted to capitals). In case the pattern is matched in a packet, an extra case-insensitive search should be made at the index where the pattern was found. Similarly, if two patterns share the same final state, they need to be verified in case of a match.

Each GPU thread processes a different reassembled network packet. We use an array to store the network packets; every time the array fills up, it is transferred to the GPU and processed at once. **Figure 4** shows the sustained throughput when matching full-size packets (i.e., of 1500-bytes length) on a single GTX770, for a varied number of packets that are processed at once. The traffic is generated from a separate machine over four 10 Gbit/s network cards. As can be shown, the AC-Full achieves a peak performance of 21.1 Gbit/s, while the AC-Compact about 16.4 Gbit/s. In both cases, all data transferring costs to and from the GPU are included. The corresponding CPU implementation achieves a performance of 0.6 Gbit/s for the AC-Full implementation, and thus a single GPU instance corresponds to 36.2 and 28.1 CPU-cores for the AC-Full and AC-Compact implementations, respectively.

As expected, AC-Full outperforms AC-Compact in all cases. The added overhead of the extra computation that AC-Compact performs in every transition decreases its performance about 30%. The main advantage of AC-Compact is that it has significantly lower memory consumption than AC-Full. The corresponding memory requirements for storing the detection engines of a single Snort instance are shown in **Table 1**. As shown, AC-Compact utilizes up to 36 times less memory, which makes it a better fit for a multi-CPU environment, due to CUDA's limitation of allocating a separate memory context for each host thread. Using AC-Compact, a single GTX770 card can store the detection engines of about 80 Snort instances (80×24.18 MB ≈ 1.9 GB). The remaining memory can be used for storing the actual contents of the incoming network packets. If AC-Full is used, only two instances can fit in device memory.

2.1.2 Compiling PCRE regular expressions to DFA state tables

The majority of tools that use regular expressions typically convert them into DFAs [5]. To do that, the most common approach is to first compile them into NFAs, and then convert them into DFAs. We also follow the same approach, and, using the Thompson algorithm [6], we first convert each regular expression into an NFA. The generated NFA is then converted incrementally to an equivalent DFA, using the Subset

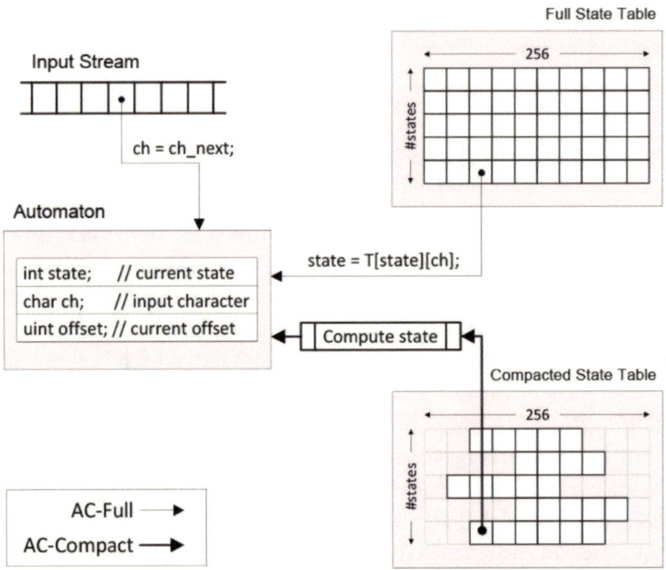

Figure 3.
State tables of AC-Full vs. AC-Compact.

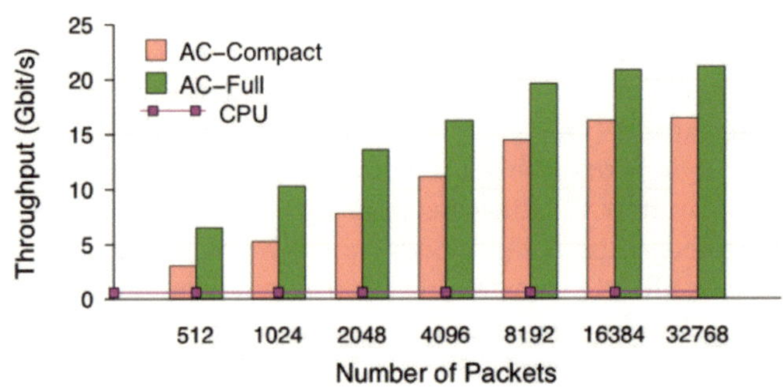

Figure 4.
GPU throughput for AC-Full and AC-Compact.

Construction algorithm. The basic concept of subset construction is to define a DFA in which each state is a set of states of the corresponding NFA. Each state in the DFA represents a set of active states in which the corresponding NFA can be in after some transition. During the matching phase, the resulting DFA achieves $O(1)$ computational cost for each incoming character.

However, a major concern when converting regular expressions into DFAs is the state-space explosion that may occur during compilation [7]. To distinguish among the states, a different DFA state may be required for all possible NFA states. Obviously, this can result to exponential growth of memory utilization, primarily due to the usage of wildcards, e.g. (.*), and repetition expressions, e.g. (a (x,y)). As a result, certain regular expressions may end-up consuming large amounts of memory when compiled to DFAs. A theoretical worst-case study shows that a single regular expression of length n can be expressed as a DFA of up to $O(\Sigma^n)$ states, where Σ is the size of the alphabet, i.e. 2^8 symbols for the extended ASCII character set [8].

To prevent the greedy memory consumption that can be occurred by some regular expressions, we follow a hybrid approach, in which we convert only the regular expressions that do not exceed a certain threshold of states; the remaining regular expressions will be matched on the CPU using NFAs. The total number of states is traced during the incremental conversion from the NFA to the DFA and the conversion stops if a certain threshold is reached. As we have experimentally found, more than 97% of the total regular expressions used by Snort can be converted to DFAs, when using an upper bound of 5000 states per expression. The remaining expressions can be processed by the CPU using an NFA implementation, similar to the vanilla Snort.

Each DFA is represented as a two-dimensional array that is mapped linearly on the memory space of the GPU. The dimensions of the array are equal to the number of states and the size of the alphabet (256 in our case), respectively. Each cell contains the next state to move to, as well as an indication of whether the state is a final state or not. The final states are represented as negative numbers, due to the fact that transition numbers can be positive integers only. Whenever the state machine reaches into a state that is represented by a negative number, it considers it as a final state and reports a match at the current input offset.

2.1.3 Multi-GPU support

Our system is able to utilize several GPUs simultaneously, by dividing the incoming flows equally and performing the signature matching concurrently across all devices. In the CUDA runtime system, each device is bound to a single process. As such, several host processes must be spawned (at least one process per device) in order to enable multi-GPU support. The load balancing scheme shown in **Figure 2** ensures that each process receives a uniform amount of flows; as a result, flows are equally distributed to the different GPUs. By default, our system utilizes all the GPUs that are available in the system, still this can be easily configured by defining the number of GPUs it should try to use.

3. Host-based virus scanning

Antivirus software is one of the most popular tools for detecting and stopping malicious or unwanted software. ClamAV [9] is a popular open-source virus scanner, which contains more than 60 thousand signatures, formed by both fixed strings, as well as regular expressions. It can be used both at the server-side for protecting mail and file servers, as well as for client personal computers. The database includes signatures for polymorphic viruses in regular expression format and for non-polymorphic viruses in simple string format. To detect non-polymorphic viruses, the current version of ClamAV uses an optimized version of the Boyer-Moore algorithm [10] for matching simple fixed string signatures. For polymorphic viruses, ClamAV uses a variant of the classical Aho-Corasick algorithm [3].

The main design principle of our GPU-assisted antivirus is to utilize the GPU in order to quickly filter out the data segments that do not contain any viruses. To achieve this, we have modified ClamAV, such that the input data stream is initially scanned by the GPU. The GPU uses a prefix of each virus signature to quickly filter-out clean data. The motivation behind this is that the majority of the data do not contain any viruses, as such the GPU filtering is quite efficient, as shown in **Figure 5**.

Figure 6 presents the overall architecture of our GPU-assisted antivirus tool. The contents of each file are read from disk and stored into a file buffer. The file buffer is used to store the contents of many files, and is transferred to the GPU in a single transaction. This results in a reduction of I/O transactions over the PCI Express bus. Moreover, the file buffer is page-locked (i.e., it does not get swapped), hence it can be transferred asynchronously, via DMA (Direct Memory Access), to the memory space of the GPU.

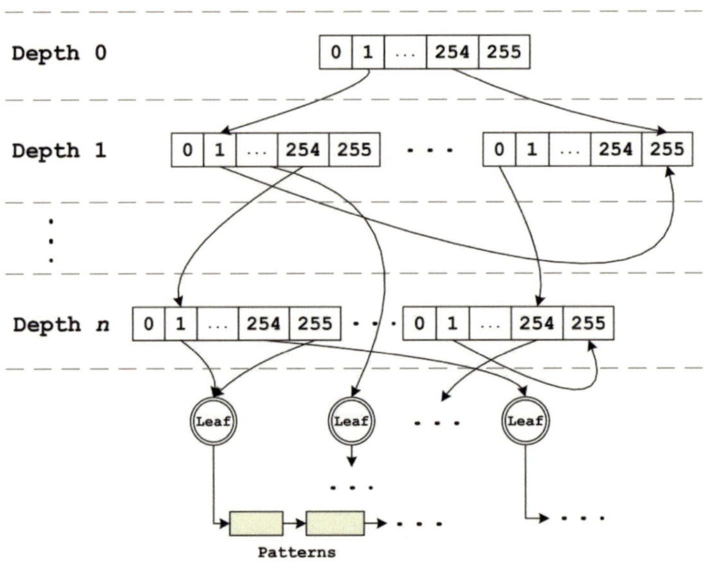

Figure 5.
Number of matches.

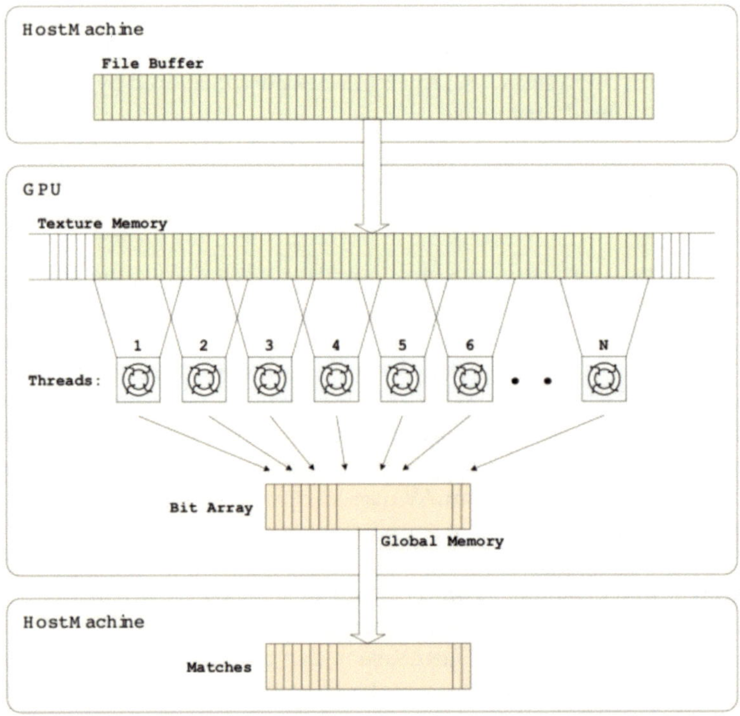

Figure 6.
The architecture of the GPU-assisted antivirus. Files are mapped onto pinned memory that can be copied onto the graphics card via DMA. A first-pass filtering is performed on the GPU and return any potential true positives for further checking onto the CPU.

Every time the GPU detects a suspicious virus, i.e., there is a prefix match, the file is further investigated by the verification module. Otherwise, no further computation takes place. The data parallel operation of the GPU is ideal for creating multiple search engine instances that will scan for virus signatures on different data in a massively parallel fashion. Overall, the GPU is employed as a high-speed first-pass filter, before completing any further potential signature-matching work on the CPU.

3.1 Basic mechanisms

Initially, the entire signature set of ClamAV is preprocessed, in order to construct a deterministic finite automaton (DFA). As we have explained before, the DFA state machine provides linear complexity over the input text stream, which is very efficient. Unfortunately, it is not feasible to construct the full DFA, due to the big number and large size of the virus signatures contained in the ClamAV.

To overcome this, we use a portion from each virus signature for constructing the DFA, and specifically only the first n symbols, similar to [11]. By doing so, the height of the resulting DFA machine is limited, as shown in **Figure 7**. Any patterns that share the same prefix are stored under the same final node, called leaf. In case the length of the signature pattern is smaller than the prefix length, the entire pattern is added. A prefix may also contain special characters, such as the wild-characters * and ?, that are used in ClamAV signatures to describe a known virus.

At the scanning phase, the input file data will be first scanned by the DFA running on the GPU. It is clear that the DFA may not be able to match an exact virus signature inside a data stream, as in most cases the length of the signature is longer than the length of the prefix we used to create the automaton. This will be the first-level filtering though, which purpose is to use the high parallelism of the GPU to quickly filter-out the majority number of true negatives, and drastically eliminate a significant portion of the input data that need to be scanned by the CPU. Obviously, the longer the prefix, the fewer the number of false positives at this initial scanning phase. As shown in **Figure 5**, using a value of 8 for n, can result to less than 0.0001% of false positives in a realistic corpus of binary files.

3.2 Parallelizing DFA matching on the GPU

During scan time, the algorithm iterates over the input data stream one byte at a time and moves the current state appropriately. The pattern matching is performed byte-wise, meaning that we have an input width of 8 bits and an alphabet size of $2^8 = 256$. Thus, each state will contain 256 transitions to other states, as shown in **Figure 7**. If the scanning algorithm reaches a final-state, then a potential signature

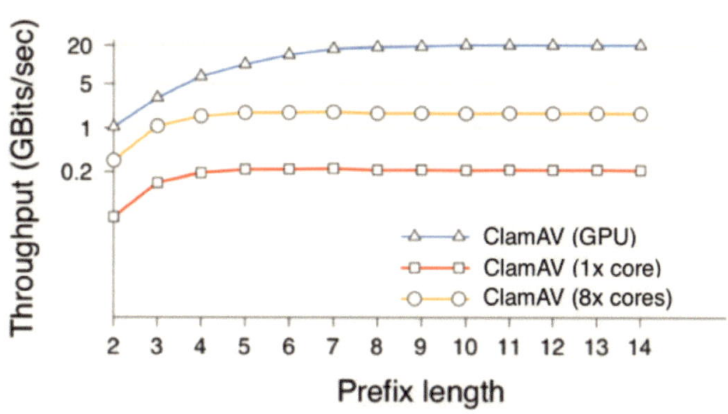

Figure 7.
A fragment of the DFA structure with n levels. All the patterns that begin with the same prefix are listed under the same leaf (final node).

match has been found, and the corresponding offset is marked. All marked offsets will be verified later by the CPU.

To utilize all streaming processors of the GPU, we exploit its data parallel capabilities by creating multiple threads. An important design decision is the partitioning of the input data to each thread. The simplest approach would be to use multiple data input streams, one for each thread, in separate memory areas. However, this will result in asymmetrical processing effort for each processor and will not scale well. For example, if the sizes of the input streams vary, the amount of work per thread will not be the same. This means that threads will have to wait, until all have finished searching the data stream that was assigned to them. To overcome this, we use a single input data stream and each thread searches a different portion of it. In particular, our strategy splits the input stream in distinct chunks, and each chunk is processed by a different thread. **Figure 8** shows how each GPU thread scans its assigned chunk, using the underlying DFA state table. Although they access the same automaton, each thread maintains its own state, eliminating any need for communication between them.

The two operations of DFA matching, is determining the address of the next state in the state table and fetching the next state from the device memory. These memory transfers can take up to several hundreds of nanoseconds, depending on the memory congestion. To obtain the highest level of performance and hide memory latencies, we run many threads in parallel. Multiple threads can overlap data transfer with computation, hence improving the memory bandwidth.

Moreover, we have explored storing the DFA state table both in the global memory space, as well as in the texture memory space of the GPU. The texture memory can be accessed in a random fashion for reading, in contrast to global memory, where the access patterns must be coalesced. This feature can be very useful for algorithms like DFA matching, which exhibit irregular access patterns across large data sets. As described in Section 2.1.2, the usage of texture memory can boost the computational throughput up to a factor of two.

A case that requires special consideration though, is when patterns span across two or more different chunks. The simplest approach for fixed string patterns, is to continue the scanning to the next chunk (s), up to n bytes, where n is the maximum pattern length in the dictionary. However, the patterns used for virus scanning are typically very large, especially compared with other signature-based tools, such as Snort. Besides that, a virus signature may contain wild card characters (i.e., *), as such the length of the patterns may not be determined. To overcome this, the following heuristic is used: each thread carries on the search to the consecutive bytes of the following chunk, up till a fail or final-state is reached. While matching a pattern that spans chunk boundaries, the state machine will perform regular transitions. However, if the state machine reaches a fail or final-state, then it is clear that there is no need to continue the searching, since any consecutive patterns will be found by the thread that was assigned to search the current chunk. This enables us to avoid any communication between the threads concerning boundaries in the input data buffer. Every time a match is found, it is stored to a bit array. The size of the bit array is equal to the size of the data that is processed at once, and each bit represents whether a match was found in the corresponding offset.

Figure 9 shows the throughput achieved for different prefix lengths. As input data stream, we use the files under /usr/bin/ of a typical Linux installation, which contains 1516 binary files of about 132 MB. To eliminate disk latencies, all files are cached in memory by the operating system. Even though the files do not contain any viruses, they exercise most code branches of our tool. As we can see, the overall

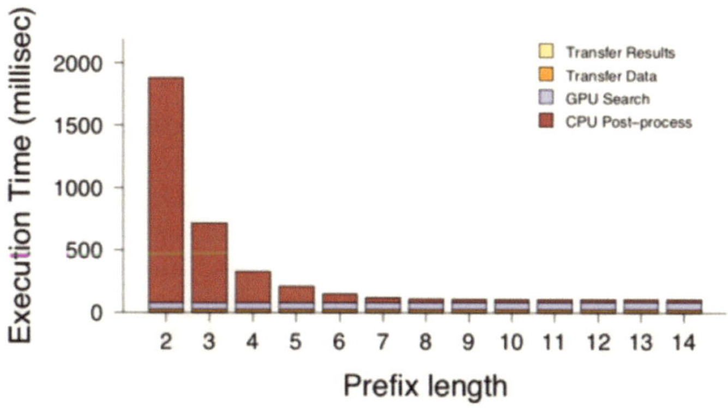

Figure 8.
Virus matching on the GPU.

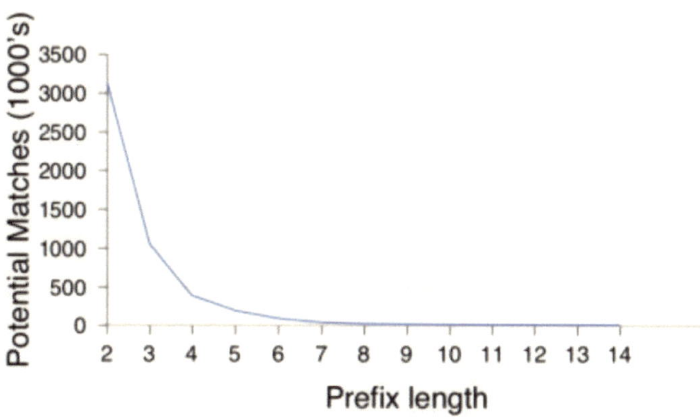

Figure 9.
Performance of GPU-assisted ClamAV and vanilla ClamAV. The performance number for ClamAV running on eight cores is also included. The CPU-only performance is still an order of magnitude less than the GPU-assisted.

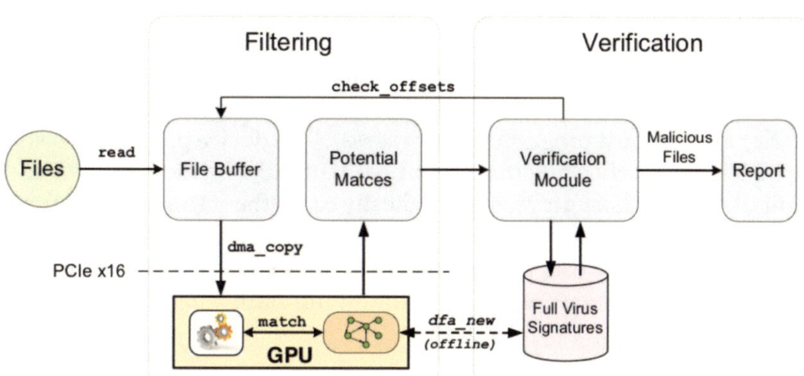

Figure 10.
Execution time breakdown.

throughput increases rapidly at a maximum of 20 Gbits/s. Moreover, the overall application throughput increases proportionally to the prefix length, due to the fact that the number of potential matches decreases, resulting to lower CPU post-processing. A plateau is reached for a prefix length of around 10 (**Figure 7**).

4. Kernel integrity monitoring

In this section, we describe how to leverage modern GPUs as a memory monitoring mechanism. In particular, we show the design of an external, snapshot-based, GPU-based kernel integrity tool that can be deployed in commodity servers and personal computers. Typically, a host memory integrity monitor should meet at least the following set of requirements [12, 13]: (i) Independence: the monitor needs to use a dedicated GPU that is completely isolated from the host. Our integrity monitor should operate continuously and detect any malicious action, notwithstanding the running state of the host machine. The GPU must be used exclusively for memory monitoring. Obviously, other usages can be served by any extra GPUs, if necessary, without affecting the proper usage of the kernel monitor. (ii) Host-memory access: the physical memory of the host must be accessed directly, in order to periodically check its integrity and detect any suspicious or malicious actions. (iii) Sufficient computational and memory resources: the system must be able to perform any requested computational operations and be capable to process large amounts of data efficiently. In addition, it must have sufficient on-chip memory that can be used for private calculations and ensure that secret data would not be leaked or held by an adversary that has compromised the host system. (iv) Out-of-band reporting: the system must be able to report the state of the host system over a secure channel. This can be achieved by establishing a secure connection that can be used to exchange valid reports, even in the case the host system has been fully compromised.

In order to meet the above requirements, several characteristics of the GPU's execution model require careful consideration. For instance, the typical GPU model in which a GPU kernel run for a while, perform some computations and then terminate cannot be considered secure. Instead, the coprocessor needs to execute in isolation, without being influenced by the host it protects. It is clear that leveraging GPUs for designing an independent environment with unrestricted memory access that will monitor the host's memory securely, is rather challenging. Many GPU characteristics must be considered carefully and in a particular way (**Figure 10**).

Figure 11 shows the overall architecture. In essence, the GPU continuously investigates, in terms of security, the specified kernel memory regions via DMA, over the PCI Express bus, and reports any suspicious or unwanted activity to an externally-connected admin station on the local network. From a high-level perspective, our system has two main parts that run in parallel: the device program (GPU code) and the host program (user process). The device program is responsible for continuously checking the integrity of requested memory regions and report any alerts. The host program periodically reads the status area and reports to the admin station, in the form of keep-alive messages. The only trusted component is hosted on the GPU; the user process cannot be trusted, so there is an end-to-end encryption scheme between the GPU and the admin station to protect against attacks.

4.1 Autonomous GPU execution

Given that the host system may be vulnerable and could be compromised, it is important that the integrity monitoring of the operating system be completely isolated from the host, and guarantee that an adversary cannot tamper any code or data used by our system. Modern GPU chips follow a non-preemptive, cooperatively scheduled, execution style, which means that only a single kernel can run on the device at any point in time. As such, a bootstrapping method is employed that

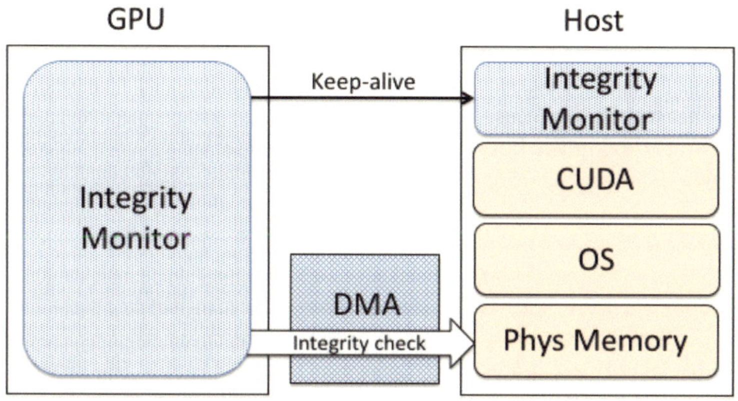

Figure 11.
The GPU-assisted integrity monitor architecture. The GPU continuously checks the integrity of host memory regions by accessing the corresponding device virtual addresses. To defend against man-in-the-middle and replay attacks on the reporting channel, a user program periodically sends an encrypted sequence number together with a status code to a separate admin station.

forbids any external interaction with our system. Any attempt to kill, pause, or suspend the GPU component of our system results in system shutdown, and the system can only resume its operation by repeating the bootstrap process. Even though many recent NVIDIA models conditionally support concurrent kernel execution, these conditions can be easily adjusted, by occupying occupy all resources. By doing so, no other, possibly malicious, code can run in parallel.

Even though these procedures ensure that our system can be initialized and run safely, current GPGPU frameworks (i.e., CUDA and OpenCL) do not support isolated and/or independent execution. To make matters worse, some drivers would even suspend a context in case the GPU kernel appears to be unresponsive. To overcome these issues, we configure the driver to ignore these types of checks. In addition, we create a second stream dedicated to the GPU kernel of our system, since by default, only one queue, or stream in CUDA terminology, is active and the host cannot issue any data transfers before the previous kernel execution is finished. Therefore, all data communications with the host and the admin station are issued over a separate stream.

4.2 Host memory access

An important requirement for our GPU-assisted kernel integrity monitor is to implement a mechanism to access the requested memory pages that need to be monitored. Current GPGPU frameworks, such as CUDA and OpenCL, use a virtual address layer that is located within the host process virtual memory. Given that our system needs to access the kernel's memory, the kernel memory regions that are monitored should be mapped to the user process.

Typically, the access of memory regions that have not been assigned to a process is prohibited in the majority of modern OSes, including Linux and Windows. Every time a process accesses a page outside of its virtual address space, a segmentation violation will be thrown. To overcome such restrictions and be able to access the memory regions where the OS kernel text and data reside, we first need to map them to the user-space of the host process that has spawned the GPU kernel. To overcome the protection added by the OS, a separate loadable kernel module is used, which is able to map a requested memory region to the user-space. These memory regions can subsequently be registered to the GPU address space, using the CUDA API. Afterwards, the GPU is able to access the requested kernel memory regions directly, through the physical address space, due to the fact that the GPU is a peripheral PCIe device (i.e., it only uses physical addressing to access the host memory). This feature enables us to un-map the user-space mappings of the kernel memory regions during the bootstrap phase, that would otherwise pose significant security risks.

4.2.1 Mapping kernel memory to GPU

During bootstrapping, our GPU-assisted integrity monitor acquires the kernel memory regions that need to be monitored. Given that these regions are located in the kernel virtual address space, the first step is to map them to the virtual address space of the user process, which spawns the execution of the kernel integrity monitoring GPU kernel.

In most modern operating systems, a peripheral device is able to bypass the virtual address layer and access physical addresses directly. The device driver creates a device-specific mapping of the device's address space that points to the corresponding host's physical pages. In order to map the corresponding kernel physical memory mappings to the GPU, we use a separate loadable kernel module that is responsible to provide the required page table mapping functionality. **Figure 12** shows the steps for mapping the OS kernel memory to the GPU. In step 1, the loadable kernel module resolves the physical mapping for a given kernel virtual address. In step 2, the kernel module allocates one page in the user context and saves its physical mapping; then it makes the allocated page point to the same page as the kernel virtual address by duplicating the PTE in the user-page table. Afterwards, in step 3, the kernel module maps this user page to the GPU (cudaHostRegister() with the cudaHostRegister-Mapped flag) and gets its device pointer via the cudaHostGetDevicePointer(). Last, the original physical mapping of the allocation is restored-and-freed by the kernel module (step 4). By doing so, any OS kernel memory page can be effectively mapped to the GPU address space. Furthermore, by un-mapping the user-allocated page right after the successful execution of the bootstrapping process, all intermediate mappings are destroyed. The same procedure is performed for all kernel virtual memory ranges that need to be monitored by our tool. The GPU driver populates a device-resident page table for the device in order to resolve its virtual addresses and spawn DMA transactions.

Finally, we compile Linux with the CONFIG_KALLSYMS_ALL = y and CONFIG_KALLSYMS = y flags, in order to have full access to the /proc./kallsyms interface. Even though this is not an inherent constraint for our design, it makes

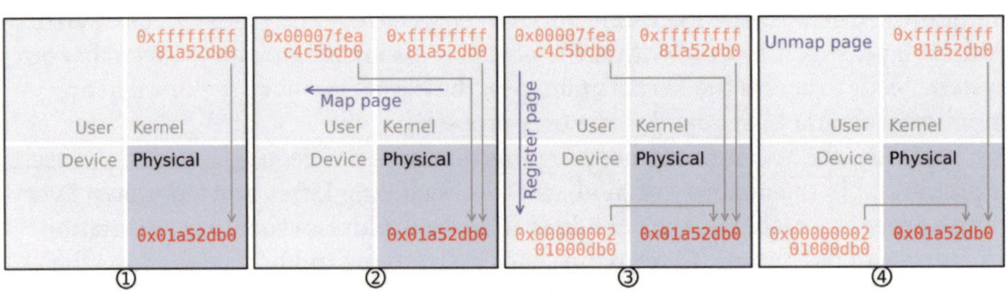

Figure 12.
Mapping OS kernel memory to the GPU. First, we have a kernel virtual address pointing to a physical address (step 1). In step 2 this mapping is duplicated to user space using a specialized kernel module capable to manipulate page tables. The user virtual address is then passed to a CUDA API call that pins the page into memory and creates the GPU-side page table entries (step 3). Finally, the intermediate user space mappings are destroyed (step 4), while the GPU continues to access the physical page.

the development and debugging much easier because it alleviates the need of custom memory scanners to search for the kernel page table address that need to be monitored. In case the access of the kernel symbol lookup table is not acceptable (i.e., in certain environments), we could locate the corresponding memory regions either using memory pattern scanners for dynamic loadable parts or via an external symbol table.

4.3 Memory integrity monitoring

The user can specify which host memory regions will be monitored; these regions can include, among others, pages that contain kernel text, kernel modules (LKM), and arrays or structures that contain function pointers (e.g., jump tables). Even though the hashing of static kernel text parts or loaded LKMs is straightforward, still many parts of the OS kernel are quite dynamic. For instance, the data structures of the VFS layer change every time a new filesystem is mounted or unmounted. In addition, function pointers can be added dynamically by every loaded LKM.

As modern GPUs offer general purpose programmability, it is feasible to implement multi-step checks on different memory regions. These checks can be quite complex, such as for example in cases where several memory pointers need to be dereferenced in order to acquire a proper kernel memory address. Such type of checks can be supported by walking the kernel page table and resolving their virtual addresses dynamically from the GPU. Given that we can already access the parts of the page table needed to follow a specific virtual address down to a leaf page table entry (PTE), we end up with a physical page number.

Finally, we note that dynamic page table resolutions are not currently supported; instead, we need to provide a static list of kernel memory regions. Still, this is not an inherent limitation of a PCIe device, such as the GPU. The development of open-source frameworks (e.g., Gdev [14]) and drivers (e.g. Nouveau [15], PSCNV [16], etc.) will make the mapping of any physical page in the GPU address space feasible.

4.4 Sufficient resources

Modern GPUs are usually equipped with hundreds of cores and adequate amount of memory. This gives the ability to keep a sufficient number of memory snapshots and much state to detect complex, multi-step, attacks. It is clear though that these types of checks can become quite sophisticated, principally due to the lack of a generic framework that will give the opportunity to define detection modules on top of our architecture. Even though the support of such complicated memory checks is not supported currently by our GPU-assisted integrity tool, still we have tested the operation of aggressively reading and hashing memory, and as we demonstrate below, the GPU prevails the computational and memory resources to support them.

In particular, we measure the detection rate of a self-hiding LKM that is loaded, repeatedly, 100 times, using a different snapshot frequency. The self-hiding LKM acts similar to the operation of a rootkit, however it does not perform any malicious operations; instead, an actual rootkit will be exposed to the monitor for a longer time period, once loaded, in order to perform its malicious actions. The detection rate achieved is shown in **Figure 13**. We utilize a GTX770 under each configuration and use the CRC-32 for checksums (as defined by ISO 3309), due to its simplicity, speed, and its wide adoption. As can be shown, we can reliably detect (i.e., 100% detection rate) that a new kernel module has been loaded before hiding itself with a snapshot frequency of 9 KHz or more.

Next, we study the implications of requiring a snapshot frequency of at least 9 KHz for accurate detection, with respect to the amount of memory we can cover. The snapshot frequency is a function of the number and size of the monitored memory regions. We notice that the memory alignment is major factor that significantly affects the performance of memory reads of the GPU; the most efficient memory reads are achieved with 16-byte aligned reads (or one uint4 in CUDA's device native data types). Unfortunately, since we cannot control how the kernel data structures will be placed in memory, we assume that many of our monitored regions will require one or two extra fetches.

In our final experiment, we focus on monitoring single memory pointer (8-bytes each). As shown in **Figure 14**, we can monitor at most 8 K pointers simultaneously without any loss in accuracy, due to the fact that we need to stay above the 9 KHz snapshot frequency. Obviously, this limits the amount of memory that we can monitor using our system, albeit 8 K addresses that are spread out in memory could potentially safeguard many important kernel data structures.

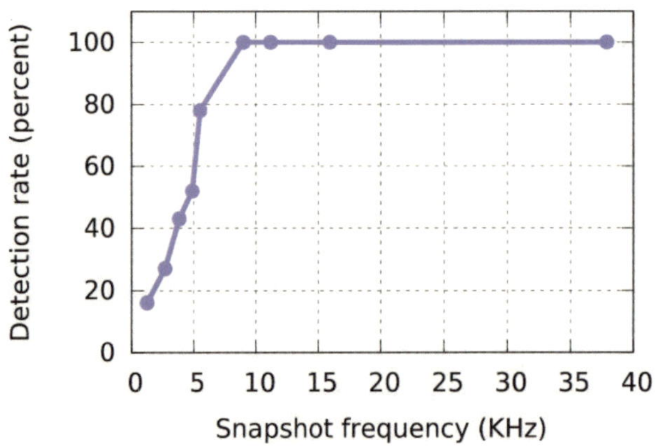

Figure 13.
Self-hiding LKM loading detection with different snapshot frequencies. For each case, a module is loaded that deletes itself from the kernel modules list 100 times, while monitoring the head of the list. A 100% detection rate with a snapshot frequency of 9 KHz or more is achieved.

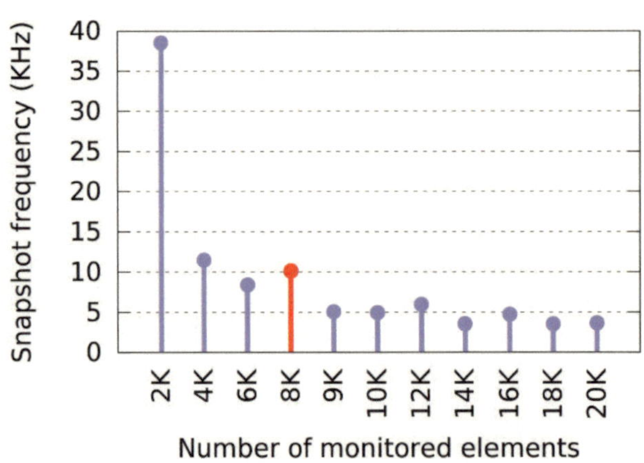

Figure 14.
Maximum achieved frequency according to the number of pointers being monitored. As the number of (8-byte) memory regions increases, the snapshot frequency decreases. A threshold of 9 KHz is required to accurately detect a self-hiding LKM loading, which is achieved with monitoring 8 K pointers.

4.5 Out-of-band execution

The coprocessor nature of GPUs offers limited defenses against itself. For instance, an attacker that has gained access on the host system can easily reset or disable the GPU device, and as a result, block its operation as integrity monitor. To solve this, an admin station needs to be deployed, completely isolated from the monitored system, that is responsible for keeping track of its proper state. Specifically, the user program that has spawned the GPU kernel that performs the integrity monitor, periodically sends keep-alive messages to the admin station via a virtual private connection. It is clear that simply sending messages to raise an alert is unsafe, due to the difficulty of the admin station to distinguish normal operation from a network partition or other failure. As such, we use keep-alive messages that encapsulate a GPU-generated status. In order to prevent attackers to send spoofed messages or replay old ones, we further encrypt the keep-alive messages together with a sequence number. Eventually, the secure channel between the admin station and the host is established at the bootstrapping phase. On the admin station, the reports are logged and is responsible that for the responsiveness of the monitor. Every time an alert is received or on the admin station, it takes the appropriate action. Moreover, the admin station takes care for any error case, such as missed reports (initiated by a time-out) or invalid messages.

Acknowledgements

The author would like to thank Sotiris Ioannidis, Michalis Polychronakis, Elias Athanasopoulos, and Lazaros Koromilas for their invaluable support and contributions during the development of several parts of this work. I gratefully acknowledge the support of NVIDIA Corporation with the donation of the Titan Xp GPU used for this research.

Author details

Giorgos Vasiliadis
Foundation for Research and Technology—Hellas, Heraklion, Crete, Greece

*Address all correspondence to: gvasil@ics.forth.gr

References

[1] Snort—Network Intrusion Detection & Prevention System. Available from: https://www.snort.org/

[2] Paxson V, Asanović K, Dharmapurikar S, Lockwood J, Pang R, Sommer R, et al. Rethinking hardware support for network analysis and intrusion prevention. In: Proceedings of the 1st USENIX Workshop on Hot Topics in Security (HotSec). 2006

[3] Aho AV, Corasick MJ. Efficient string matching: An aid to bibliographic search. Communications of the ACM. 1975;**18**(6):333-340

[4] Norton M. Optimizing Pattern Matching for Intrusion Detection. Whitepaper. 2004. Available from: https://www.snort.org/documents/optimization-of-pattern-matches-for-ids

[5] PCRE: Perl Compatible Regular Expressions. Available from: http://www.pcre.org

[6] Thompson K. Programming techniques: Regular expression search algorithm. Communications of the ACM. 1968;**11**(6):419-422

[7] Berry G, Sethi R. From regular expressions to deterministic automata. Theoretical Computer Science. 1986;**48**(1):117-126

[8] Hopcroft JE, Ullman JD. Introduction to Automata Theory, Languages, and Computation. Boston, MA, USA: Addison-Wesley Longman Publishing Co., Inc.; 1990

[9] ClamAV Open-source Antivirus. Available from: http://www.clamav.net/

[10] Boyer RS, Moore JS. A fast string searching algorithm. Communications of the Association for Computing Machinery. 1977;**20**(10):762-772

[11] Miretskiy Y, Das A, Wright CP, Zadok E. Avfs: An on-access anti-virus file system. In: Proceedings of the 13th USENIX Security Symposium. 2004

[12] Petroni NL Jr, Fraser T, Molina J, Arbaugh WA. Copilot: A coprocessor-based kernel runtime integrity monitor. In: USENIX Security Symposium. 2004

[13] Lee H, Moon H, Jang D, Kim K, Lee J, Paek Y, et al. KI-mon: A hardware-assisted event-triggered monitoring platform for mutable kernel object. In: USENIX Security Symposium. 2013

[14] shinpei0208/gdev. Available from: https://github.com/shinpei0208/gdev

[15] Nouveau driver for nVidia cards. Available from: http://nouveau.freedesktop.org/

[16] PathScale NVIDIA graphics driver. Available from: https://github.com/pathscale/pscnv

Chapter 5

Particle-Based Fused Rendering

Koji Koyamada and Naohisa Sakamoto

Abstract

In this chapter, we propose a fused rendering technique that can integrally handle multiple irregular volumes. Although there is a strong requirement for understanding large-scale datasets generated from coupled simulation techniques such as computational structure mechanics (CSM) and computational fluid dynamics (CFD), there is no fused rendering technique to the best of our knowledge. For this purpose, we can employ the particle-based volume rendering (PBVR) technique for each irregular volume dataset. Since the current PBVR technique regards an irregular cell as a planar footprint during depth evaluation, the straightforward employment causes some artifacts especially at the cell boundaries. To solve the problem, we calculate the depth value based on the assumption that the opacity describes the cumulative distribution function (CDF) of a probability variable, w, which shows a length from the entry point in the fragment interval in the cell. In our experiments, we applied our method to numerical simulation results in which two different irregular grid cells are defined in the same space and confirmed its effectiveness with respect to the image quality.

Keywords: volume rendering, irregular volume, unstructured grid

1. Introduction

Coupled analysis is important to solve complex phenomena. Several computational schemes such as computational fluid dynamics (CFD), computational structure mechanics (CSM), and computational electronic magnetics (CEM) are applied to the same geometrical domain, and high-performance computing (HPC) facility has been used for the computation. Since, in general, the requirement for the computational grid is different at each scheme, and the space is composed of multiple irregular volumes. Thus, a volume rendering technique which can handle multiple irregular volumes is expected.

Volume rendering can provide useful information because with this technique, it is possible to grasp the spatial distribution of the related physical quantities. It is a powerful technique for displaying volume datasets, especially three-dimensional scalar data fields, which are composed of scalar data values defined in three-dimensional space. In a CSM, CFD or CEM simulation, the three-dimensional space is composed of computational cells, the shapes of which are, for example, tetrahedra, prisms, and hexahedra. In a large-scale simulation model for complex physical phenomena, the number of computational cells may be more than one million.

Current volume rendering techniques require discrete sampling in which the composition is executed in the visibility order. In the volume rendering calculation, accumulating the optical depth is time consuming. The optical depth is accumulated so that we can efficiently calculate the occlusion of the scattered light from various lighting positions. Most volume rendering techniques accumulate the optical depth in order from front to back or from back to front along a viewing ray.

Although this sorted sampling is straightforward in structured grid data, it becomes more complicated if the computation is conducted in a distributed computing environment. In such an environment, the sub-volume dataset is stored in each distributed node. In this case, it is difficult for a sub-volume to be sorted along the viewing ray since the shape of the sub-volume may be concave. On the other hand, the shape of a computational cell is convex. The whole volume is subdivided into multiple sub-volumes so that the total data transmission cost is minimized.

To handle the problem, a particle-based rendering technique, which does not need visibility sorting, has been proposed [1]. In this technique, opaque emissive particles are employed for realizing sorting-free rendering. There are two approaches for the implementation, that is, an object-space approach and an image-space approach (see **Figure 1**). In the former approach, which we call object-space particle-based volume rendering (O-PBVR), a particle density function is estimated from a user-specified transfer function, and a set of opaque particles are generated at each computational cell. The generated particles are projected onto an image plane, and the projection is repeated to improve the image quality. Although O-PBVR shows good scalability for handling large-scale irregular volume [2], the current drawback of the technique is the generation of low-quality images in which particles are visible on the boundary surface polygons when viewed closely. Moreover, with O-PBVR, it is necessary to generate a large number of particles to obtain a high-resolution image.

In the latter approach, we proposed a sorting-free technique by regarding the brightness equation as the expected value of the luminosity of a sampling point along a viewing ray [3]. We applied the technique to a projected tetrahedral technique with pre-integration. We called this image-space particle-based volume rendering (I-PBVR). We conducted a thorough experimental analysis to construct the performance model [3]. The model suggests that I-PBVR is preferable to O-PBVR

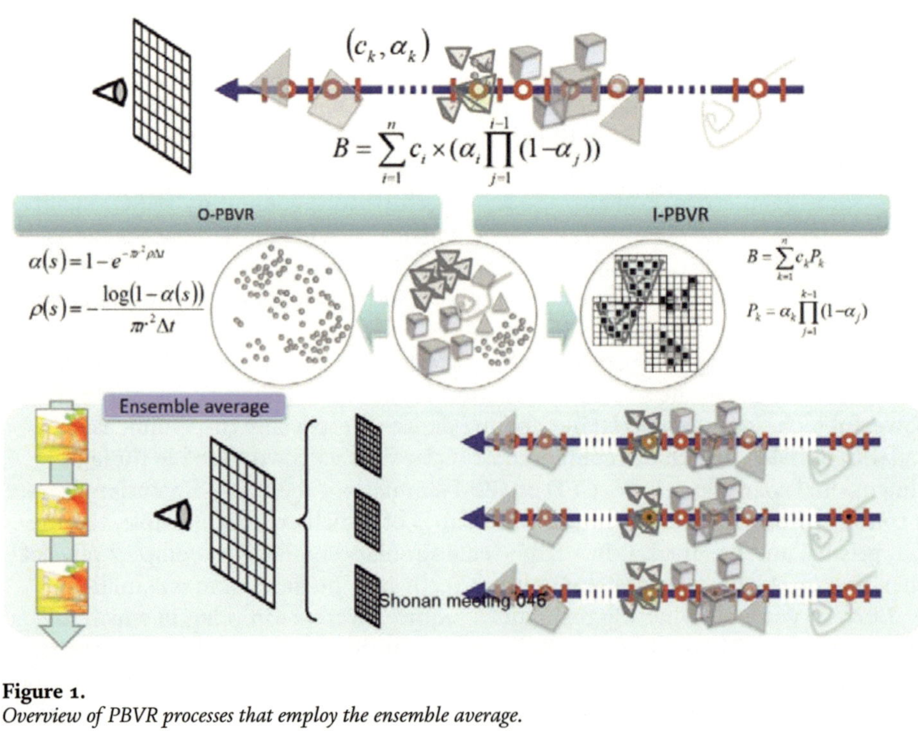

Figure 1.
Overview of PBVR processes that employ the ensemble average.

when a volume dataset is rendered in a high resolution. In addition, I-PBVR becomes a feasible choice for rendering irregular volume data when particle generation becomes frequent.

To understand the relationships between variables in the irregular volume data, it is necessary to integrate multiple volumes, into a single volume rendering. In this chapter, we improve the I-PBVR technique in terms of its extensibility to multiple volumes and propose a new technique for semi-transparent rendering which can integrally handle multiple volumes without visibility sorting. I-PBVR regards a tetrahedral cell as a triangle footprint on the image plane. When a single volume is rendered, each footprint does not intersect with the other one since the volume is composed of cells that are not overlapped with others. When multiple volumes are rendered, the footprints may intersect with others. This intersection causes a problem in which the cell boundaries are visible when dealing with multiple volumes. Thus, in this chapter, our research question is "How can we realize a fused volume rendering technique which is free from artifact?" The hypothesis to the question is "If we employ an adequate probability process to sample particles along a viewing in a grid cell, the artifact is not noticeable." In the early age of volume rendering, Blinn assumed that the number of particles is distributed in a volume space according to the Poisson distribution. If we take an interval that is a part of the viewing ray cut by cell faces, the distance between particles is distributed according to the exponent distribution.

In the remaining part, we first describe related work and the basic theory of PBVR and then propose a fused rendering technique using PBVR. Finally, we make a comparative work to confirm the effectiveness of the proposed technique. To test the hypothesis, we design the following experiments for the sampling along the interval:

1. The sampling is made at the entry, exit or middle points along an interval in the grid cell.

2. The sampling is made at a random position along an interval in the grid cell.

3. The sampling is made according to a probability process, which is determined based on an opacity along the interval.

2. Related work

In the particle-based modeling of Saturn's ring, Blinn assumed that the number of particles follows the Poisson distribution although he did not describe it in detail [4]. The assumption led to a definition of opacity which was an important keyword for the volume rendering. Then, volume rendering has been the focus of intensive study for nearly three decades [5–7]. The volume rendering of unstructured volume data has received much attention, and several approaches have been proposed. Extensive literature and surveys on volume rendering are available that address unstructured volume data [8, 9]. A concern has often been visibility sorting, which causes a severe bottleneck in the interactive exploration.

To solve the problem recognized by many volume rendering researchers, we returned to a density emitter model and presented the basic concept for this approach. The proposed PBVR technique represents the 3D scalar fields as a set of particles and considers both emission and absorption effects [1, 2]. The particle density is derived from a user-specified transfer function and is used to estimate the number of particles to be generated in a given volume dataset. Because the particles can be considered fully opaque, no visibility sorting processing is required during the rendering process, which is advantageous from a distributed processing perspective.

The development of a fused rendering technique began in the seismic or medical imaging field. Lu Cai et al. developed a fused volume rendering technique for multiple seismic attribute volume data by the way of planar slices or horizon slices and revealed a variety of geological phenomena more effectively and clearly in order to provide a true three-dimensional perspective view. Their method can address only regular volume datasets [10].

3. Particle-based volume rendering

3.1 Definition of opacity

In image generation in volume rendering, it is thought that giving a viewing ray (viewpoint and direction), when there is no other emissive particle between the particle and the viewpoint, the energy from the particle reaches the viewpoint. Let us consider a certain section on the viewing ray, where τ particles are distributed on average. Furthermore, suppose that this section is divided into M equal parts, M small sections are formed, and particles are present in k small sections. Here, it is assumed that there is at most one particle in each small section and k is a natural number in addition to 0. At this time, the probability p that there is a particle in the small section is as follows:

$$p = \frac{\tau}{M} \tag{1}$$

Such a distribution follows a binomial distribution, and its probability is given as follows:

$$P(X = k) = {}_{M}C_{k}p^{k}(1 - p)^{M-k} \tag{2}$$

Here, the number of particles X is set as a random variable. When M is brought close to infinity while keeping τ = Mp constant, its distribution becomes the Poisson distribution of the average τ. The probability that there are k particles in the section is expressed by the following equation:

$$P(N = k) = \frac{\tau^{k}e^{-\tau}}{k!} \tag{3}$$

Here, e is the Napier's constant (e = 2.71828 ...), and k! is the factorial of k. Thus, the probability is a positive real number. The Poisson distribution is often employed in the context of the number of occurrences of events within the interval defined in the time domain, but in volume rendering, it is considered not in the time domain but in the space domain. Eq. 3 represents the probability that k particles exist when the average number of particles is τ. When k = 0, it represents the situation in which no particle exists in the section on the viewing ray.

$$P(N = 0) = e^{-\tau} \tag{4}$$

If there are many particles, the rate at which energy reaches the viewpoint becomes small, and it is easier to define the passing distance of light by the number of particles rather than the actual distance. Therefore, the average particle number τ is also called the optical thickness. Additionally, a negative sign is given to this optical thickness, and an index is taken, that is, Eq. 4 is called transparency (t), and it shows the ease of light transmission. The opacity α is obtained by subtracting this transparency from 1 and represents the probability that one or more particles exist in the section.

3.2 Volume rendering

In traditional computer graphics, it is assumed that all light is radiated from the outside, the particles constituting the object are treated as reflectors, and the light scattering and absorption are repeated inside the object. On the other hand, in the volume rendering technique proposed by Sabella in 1988, the internal structure of the volume data can be known by treating the particle as a radiator in addition to a reflector (particle emission model) for the purpose of visualizing the scalar volume.

In Blinn's model and Kajiya's model, the radiant energy is only reflected from the light source and energy emission (luminescence) by the particles themselves has not been considered. However, in the model of Sabella, from the standpoint of visualizing the volume data, we assume that the particles themselves emit light.

To accurately simulate the light scattering phenomenon inside the object, complicated analysis using radiation theory becomes necessary, and it is necessary to solve the scattering equation derived from that theory. In the particle emission model, focusing only on the viewing ray direction, we use a simple equation describing the transmission of optical energy with volume data. This equation can be formulated as follows by considering the difference in radiant intensity (luminance value) B in a cylindrical tube of minute length.

$$\begin{aligned} dB(t)A &= -absorbed + emitted \\ &= (-B(t) + c(t)) \times \pi r^2 \rho(t) A dt \\ \frac{dB(t)}{dt} &= (-B(t) + c(t)) \times \pi r^2 \rho(t) \end{aligned} \tag{5}$$

Here, $\rho(t)$ is the particle density (the number of particles per unit volume), r is the particle radius, and c (t) is the light emission amount per unit area.

$$B_0 = B(t_0) = \int_{t_n}^{t_0} c(t) \times \pi r^2 \rho(t) \times \exp\left(-\int_{t}^{t_0} \pi r^2 \rho(\lambda) d\lambda\right) dt \tag{6}$$

Eq. 6 is integrated in the interval in which the parameters $t_0$and t_n represent the nearest and the farthest points, respectively, from the viewpoint among the intersection points of the volume data and the viewing ray.

This is called the brightness equation. Generally, the brightness value B and the light emission amount c (t) are composed of three components of red, green, and blue. Eq. 6 shows that energy emitted from a point on the viewing ray reaches the viewpoint by receiving attenuation represented by an exponential term. Note that the exponent term represents the optical thickness τ, so it is equal to the transparency calculated by assuming a Poisson distribution.

In the particle emission model in volume rendering, from the viewpoint of visualization of scalar data, scalar values interpolated in particle positions are converted into color data (composed of three components of red, green, and blue). This conversion table is called a transfer function together with a conversion table to opacity described below.

In volume rendering, by performing shading processing, it is possible to effectively express shading on the isosurface inherent in the scalar volume. Particularly in the case of three-dimensional medical images, it is necessary to visualize complicated structures such as bones, muscles, blood vessels, etc. as isosurfaces, and shading processing becomes important. In shading processing targeting the scalar volume data, luminance value calculation using the gradient vector obtained by interpolation calculation inside the grid cell is performed.

To numerically calculate the brightness equation represented by Eq. 6, an integration area defined on the viewing ray is divided by a step width in which particle emission can be regarded as constant.

At this time, the k-th light emission amount c (t) is regarded as a constant and is set as c_k. In the calculation of integration, the integral of the exponent part is divided into the integral section and others. For those that are divided outside the integration interval, sections corresponding to the division sections are divided and expressed with product signs. Each element of the product symbol is an index obtained by attaching a minus sign to the optical thickness and represents the transparency described above.

As a result, it can be seen that a term of the same form as the exponent term of the divided section outside the integral section and the transparency are included. Transparency takes values from 0 to 1 by definition. The value obtained by subtracting this transparency from 1 is called opacity, as mentioned above, and may be a target of transfer function, and opacity is used in volume rendering in many cases. That is, in the k-th integral interval, the opacity α_k is defined as follows.

$$\alpha_k = 1 - \exp\left(-\int_{t_k}^{t_{k-1}} \pi r^2 \rho(\lambda) d\lambda\right) = 1 - \exp\left(-\pi r^2 \rho_k \Delta t\right) \tag{7}$$

where Δt is the length of the integration interval, and ρ_k is the average particle density in the integral interval k. By introducing this opacity, Eq. 6 is as follows:

$$B_k = c_k \alpha_k \prod_{j=0}^{k-2} \left(1 - \alpha_{j+1}\right) = c_k \alpha_k \prod_{j=1}^{k-1} \left(1 - \alpha_j\right) \tag{8}$$

By adding all the terms described by Eq. 8, the brightness is as follows:

$$B = \sum_{k=1}^{n} \left[c_k \times \alpha_k \prod_{j=1}^{k-1} \left(1 - \alpha_j\right) \right] \tag{9}$$

Normally, this opacity is converted from the scalar value S in the transfer function specified by the user. That is, the opacity is a function of the scalar value S.

$$\alpha = \alpha(S(x, y, z)) \tag{10}$$

If the length of the integration interval is a value Δt‘ different from the predetermined Δt, it is necessary to make the following correction.

$$\begin{aligned} \alpha_k &= 1 - \exp\left(-\pi r^2 \rho_k \Delta t\right) \\ \alpha'_k &= 1 - \exp\left(-\pi r^2 \rho_k \Delta t'\right) \\ \therefore \alpha'_k &= 1 - \left(1 - \alpha_k\right)^{\frac{\Delta t'}{\Delta t}} \end{aligned} \tag{11}$$

In volume rendering, the user should have a large opacity (maximum value is 1.0) for the scalar value to be emphasized and a small opacity (minimum value of 0.0 for the less important scalar value) to set the transfer function. By doing so, the relationship between the scalar value and the opacity can be defined, and according to Eq. 11, the following particle density is defined in the three-dimensional region in which the volume data are defined.

$$\rho_k = \frac{\log(1-\alpha_k)}{\pi r^2 \Delta t} \tag{12}$$

Eq. 12 defines the opacity when a transfer function is set in the three-dimensional region, and the particle density is determined when the particle diameter is determined; thus, particles can be generated using an appropriate method. By allocating colors to particles and projecting them on the image plane, volume rendering can be realized.

During the exploration phase, the opacity is often modified in order to change an emphasized region. If we keep the particle radius as defined in the first place, we need to re-generate particles which requires a significant computational time. To avoid the additional particle generation process, we need to change the particle radius on the condition that the particle density stays the same. If we change the opacity from α_k to α_k', the new radius r' becomes as follows:

$$r' = r\sqrt{\frac{\log(1-\alpha_k)}{\log(1-\alpha_k')}} \tag{13}$$

3.3 O-PBVR

O-PBVR is comprised of three processes: particle generation, particle projection, and the ensemble average [1]. The first process constructs a density field and generates particles consistent with the density function. The density is derived from a user-specified transfer function that converts a scalar to an opacity data value, and it describes the probability that a particle is present at a given point in space. The second process projects particles onto an image plane, and the corresponding particle buffer stores the particles. Each pixel on the image plane contains sub-pixels (i.e., divided pixels), and the number of division is called the sub-pixel level. This sub-pixel processing is equivalent to an ensemble average which repeats the first and second processes in sequence, N times, and calculates the resulting brightness values by averaging the accumulating color values.

3.3.1 Particle generation

The particle model considers three particle attributes: shape, size, and density. The particle shape is assumed to be spherical, as in the density emitter model. The size of the sphere is characterized by its diameter, which is the same as a side length of a sub-pixel. The particle density ρ can be estimated from the user-specified transfer function. To generate a rendering image equivalent in quality to the volume ray-casting result, the above relation must estimate the particle density function. The number of particles N in a volume cell is calculated as

$$N = \int_{\text{Cell}} \rho dv \tag{14}$$

The particles are generated cell-by-cell. In each cell, particle locations are calculated stochastically in the local coordinate system, which may be one of a variety of types (e.g., barycentric coordinate). Because this technique generates particles with uniform sampling in each cell, blocky noise occurs in the rendering result. To solve this problem, Metropolis sampling for O-PBVR is presented [1]. Metropolis sampling, which uses a ratio of density at the current position to that at the candidate position, is widely used as an efficient Monte Carlo technique in chemistry and physics.

3.3.2 Particle projection

Using the aforementioned particle generation method, we can generate particles in a volume space according to the density function $\rho(x)$. By projecting these particles onto the image plane, we calculate the brightness values of the corresponding pixels. We also perform particle occlusion with the Z-buffer algorithm during this projection stage. This incorporates the effects of particle collision, which prevents some particles from reaching the image plane.

In the present method, we assume that the particles are completely opaque. Thus, neither alpha blending nor visibility ordering is required. However, when the number of projected particles is small, for instance one per pixel, it becomes difficult to produce a semi-transparent appearance. This problem can be solved by an ensemble average, that is, by accumulating a pixel value for particles generated multiple times and averaging their brightness values within the pixel.

3.4 I-PBVR

I-PBVR is comprised of three processes: cell projection, stochastic rasterization, and ensemble average. The first process decomposes a cell into several tetrahedral cells and splits each of the tetrahedral cells into a set of triangles on the projection plane. The second process renders the fragments of the triangles with a probability equal to the opacity value at each ray segment along a viewing ray. It projects particles onto the image plane, and the corresponding particle buffer stores the particles' colors and depths. The third process repeats the first and second processes in sequence, N times, and calculates the resulting brightness values by averaging the accumulating color values.

3.4.1 Cell projection

Projected tetrahedra (PT) is a technique for rendering a tetrahedral volume dataset using polygonal approximation, which regards a tetrahedral cell as triangles. In this technique, first the tetrahedral cells are sorted in the order of distance from a viewing point. Second, each tetrahedral cell is projected onto an image plane and subdivided into three or four PT triangles. In the original PT technique, the color and opacity are evaluated at the vertices and rasterizing of the PT triangle generates the fragments on the image plane. Finally, the colors are accumulated to calculate the pixel value using the back-to-front algorithm. In I-PBVR, although the particle radius is not explicitly specified, it actually becomes a pixel scale on the image plane.

To improve the accuracy of the pixel value, a pre-integration technique, proposed by Engel [11], is often employed in the rendering stage. The technique calculates the color and opacity in the ray segment in a more precise way than the conventional technique which just samples a scalar value at the middle point of the ray segment. If the color or the opacity changes drastically in the ray segment, this sampling may miss the important feature. The pre-integration assumes that the scalar is linearly distributed in the ray segment. In this assumption, the integrand can be transformed from a function of the distance to that of the scalar. The pre-integration computes the lookup tables mapping three integration parameters (scalar value at the front triangle face s_f, back one s_b, and length of the segment l in Eq. 18) to the pre-integrated color C and opacity α. By considering many combinations of scalar and distance values, the pre-integration table is stored as 3D texture in GPU.

3.4.2 Stochastic rasterization

From Eq. 9, we can regard a brightness calculation model as an expected value calculation in which there are n ray segments along a viewing ray, and the k-th particle occurs at the probability of α_k. Thus, the brightness can be regarded as the expected value of the luminosity from the ray segment:

$$B = \sum_{k=1}^{n} P_k c_k \tag{15}$$

where the possibility that the k-th luminosity c_k is equal to the brightness value can be described as follows by using the opacity value α_k:

$$P_k = \alpha_k \prod_{j=1}^{k-1} \left(1 - \alpha_j\right) \tag{16}$$

This represents an event in which there is no particle from the first to the (k-1)-th ray segment, and there is more than one particle in the k-th ray segment. In this case, the brightness B becomes c_k since opaque and emissive particles are used. Please note that the brightness is not contributed to by the ray segments from the k-th to the last segments since the (k-1)-th particle completely occludes these segments.

3.5 Ensemble average

In both O-PBVR and I-PBVR, a stochastic approach is employed to generate particles that are projected onto an image plane. The generation is repeated to make the average of the pixel values, which can be viewed as an ensemble average. An ensemble is an imaginary collection of notionally identical experiments. In the ensemble average, the total brightness is calculated by averaging the pixel values in all of the repetitions. We confirmed the fluctuation of the total brightness follows a large number and evaluated the minimum repetition, 65,536, that makes the total variance become within half of the minimum discretized brightness in the worst case [12]. This result suggests that little improvement can be expected in the brightness value when the repetition number exceeds 65,536 in most cases. When we interact the volume rendering image with some transformation such as translation, rotation, or scaling, we think much of the interaction by reducing the repetition number at the cost of the image quality. When we intend to improve the image quality, we stay still without any interaction.

4. Particle-based fused rendering

In I-PBVR, we generate a particle in an interval of a tetrahedral cell by regarding the opacity as a cumulative distribution function as shown in **Figure 2**. The opacity

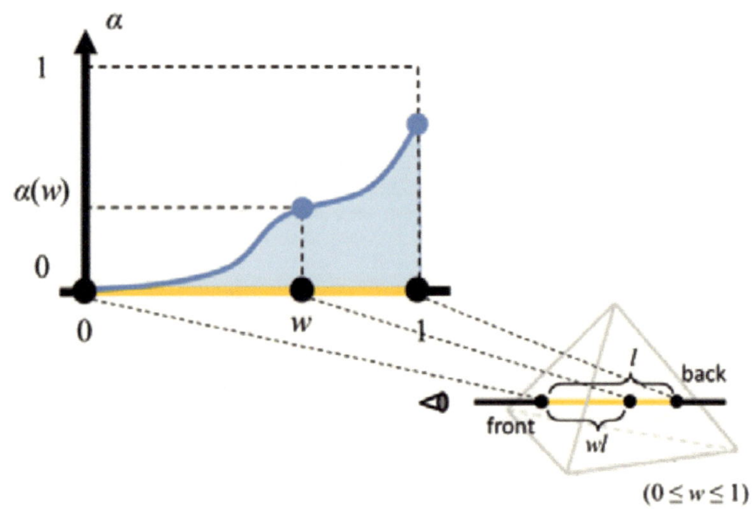

Figure 2.
Cumulative distribution function defined as the opacity between the entry point and the particle in the section where the viewing ray is cut into a tetrahedral cell.

can be represented as a function of a length from the entry point in the interval. Thus, the depth, which is the length from the entry point, can be regarded as a probability variable which follows a probability density function that is a derivative of the cumulative distribution function (CDF).

When we consider the definition of the opacity, we find that it describes the CDF of a probability variable, w, which shows a length from the entry point in the fragment interval. The probability density function, that is, its derivative, describes an exponential distribution, which matches the theorem that the number of particles follows the Poisson distribution since the exponential distribution describes the distance between particles in a Poisson process.

The opacity in Eq. 7 can be used to express the CDF α (w) of the random variable w as follows:

$$\alpha(w) = 1 - \exp\left(-\int_{t_{k-1}-wl}^{t_{k-1}} \tau(\lambda)d\lambda\right) \tag{17}$$

Let l be the width of the section where the viewing ray is cut by the cell. This equation represents the opacity calculated between the entry point and the position where the particles are located in the entry. This interval can be expressed as wl using the random variable w (see **Figure 2**). Furthermore, the theorem that the probability density function is represented by an exponential function is consistent with theorem that "when the number of particles in a certain section follows the Poisson distribution, the particle spacing follows the exponential distribution."

In the pre-integration method, the opacity in the section is described as follows.

$$\alpha(s_f, s_b, l) = 1 - \exp\left(-\frac{l}{s_b - s_f}\left(T(s_b) - T(s_f)\right)\right) \tag{18}$$

Here, s_f and s_b are scalar data values interpolated and computed at the entry and exit points of the section, respectively, and l represents the width of the section as described above. $T(\text{s})$ represents an integral expression for calculating the number of particles generated in the interval.

$$T(s) = \int_0^s \tau(\lambda) \mathrm{d}\lambda \tag{19}$$

In the proposed method, it is assumed that the scalar data value is linearly interpolated in the interval, and it is expressed as s (w) at the point expressed using the random variable w. This assumption arises from the linear distribution of scalar data in line segments defined in tetrahedrons when interpolation calculations using scalar data and volume coordinates defined at each vertex are performed in the tetrahedrons.

$$s(w) = (1 - w)s_f + ws_b \tag{20}$$

Therefore, in the case of $s_f \neq s_b$, the opacity function α (w) expressed by Eq. 17 is expressed as follows.

$$\begin{aligned} \alpha(w) &= \alpha(s_f, s(w), wl) \\ &= 1 - \exp\left(-\frac{l}{s_b - s_f}\left(T(s(w)) - T(s_f)\right)\right) \end{aligned} \tag{21}$$

In the case of $s_f = s_b$, the opacity function α (w) expressed by Eq. 17 is expressed as follows:

$$\alpha(w) = 1 - \exp\left(-\tau(s_f) \cdot wl\right) \tag{22}$$

Here, reference is made to the following derivation process.

$$\begin{aligned} \alpha(s_f, s_b, l) &= \lim_{s_f \to s_b} \alpha(s_f, s_b, l) \\ &= \lim_{s_f \to s_b} \left(1 - \exp\left(-\frac{l}{s_b - s_f}\left(T(s_b) - T(s_f)\right)\right)\right) \\ &= 1 - \exp\left(-T'(s_f) \cdot l\right) \\ &= 1 - \exp\left(-\tau(s_f) \cdot l\right) \end{aligned} \tag{23}$$

4.1 Calculation of depth value by inverse function method

In this method, particles are placed at a position wl away from the start point of the section. At this time, assuming that the random variable w follows the probability density function such that the cumulative distribution function is the opacity α(w), this variable w can be generated using the inverse function method. In the inverse function method, when the random number R exists in the range of the interval $[0, \alpha(s_f, s_b, l)]$, the variable w is calculated using Eqs. 24 or 25. Eqs. 24 and 25 are derived from Eqs. 21 and 22 when $s_f \neq s_b$ and $s_f = s_b$, respectively.

$$\begin{aligned} w &= \alpha^{-1}(R) \\ &= \frac{1}{s_b - s_f}\left(T^{-1}\left(-\frac{s_b - s_f}{l}\log(1 - R) + T(s_f)\right) - s_f\right) \end{aligned} \tag{24}$$

$$\begin{aligned} w &= \alpha^{-1}(R) \\ &= -\frac{\log(1 - R)}{\tau(s_f) \cdot l} \end{aligned} \tag{25}$$

Using Eqs. 24 and 25, we can calculate the depth value of the particle.

$$D(w) = (1 - w) \cdot D_f + w \cdot D_b \qquad (26)$$

Here, D_f and D_b represent the depth values at the start and end points of the section. Similarly, scalar data values at particle positions can be interpolated and color values can be calculated using the transfer function.

This method was implemented using OpenGL and the GPU shader described in GLSL. For the implementation of pre-integration, we used two-dimensional pre-integration to perform error correction [13] with perspective transformation, so we implemented the function T described in Eq. 19 as a two-dimensional texture in the GPU [14]. To determine the random variable w described in Eq. 20, an inverse function of T is required, but in order to realize efficient computation, the function value was calculated in advance and this was also implemented in the GPU as a two-dimensional texture.

5. Result and discussion

Experiments were conducted to evaluate the effectiveness of this method. The experiment used CPU: Intel Core i7 3.3GHz, MEM: 16GB, and GPU: Intel Iris Graphics 550.

To confirm the appropriateness of the depth value in this method, experiments were conducted on two irregular volume data consisting of a single tetrahedral cell. **Figure 3** visualizes each irregular volume data using a red/blue monochrome color map that increases the color value according to the data value.

As a comparative experiment, as in the conventional method, the depth value in the tetrahedral cell is visualized by fixing the relative position in the section like the entry point, the middle point, and the exit point. It turns out that the proposed method realizes satisfactory visualization at the intersection of the two tetrahedral lattices. According to the result of the conventional method, a change in unnatural color value can be visually confirmed.

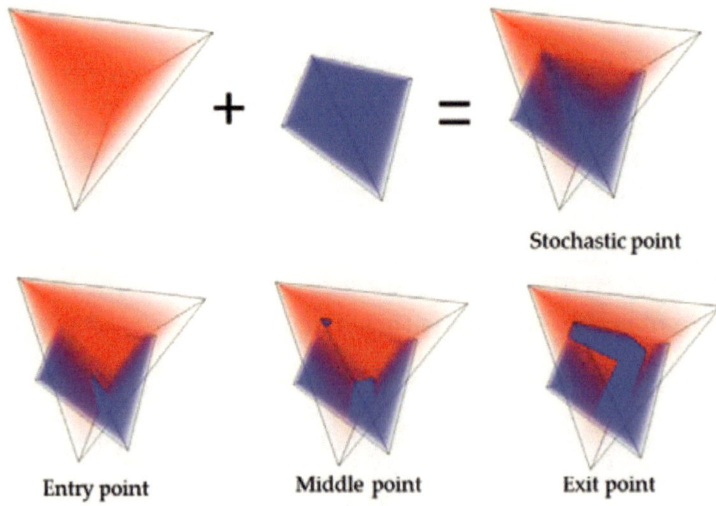

Figure 3.
Application example of proposed method for intersecting tetrahedral cell (red and blue color maps were used for each tetrahedral cell).

Experiments were conducted using two irregular volume data of appropriate size. These are obtained as a result of computational fluid dynamics calculation and are called "Tank." This calculation relates to a physical phenomenon when a pipe-like valve installed in a gas tank filled with a high-pressure state is instantly opened. Therefore, the important variables are pressure data and velocity absolute value data (both are scalar data). Pressure data and velocity absolute data were calculated using 9827 and 516 tetrahedral cells, respectively. **Figure 5** shows the volume rendering display of the fused mixed irregular volume data with different cells. In this experiment, red color is assigned to pressure data, and blue color is assigned to velocity absolute value data (**Figure 4**).

In **Figure 5**, we compare the proposed method (a), the previous methods (b), (c), and (d) in which the relative position in the section is fixed as the entry point, the middle point, and the exit point for the depth values in the tetrahedral cells and a method in which a random position is located between the entry and exit points (e). In the five figures, in addition to presenting the overall visualization result (grid line presence/absence) and the local visualization result (grid line presence/

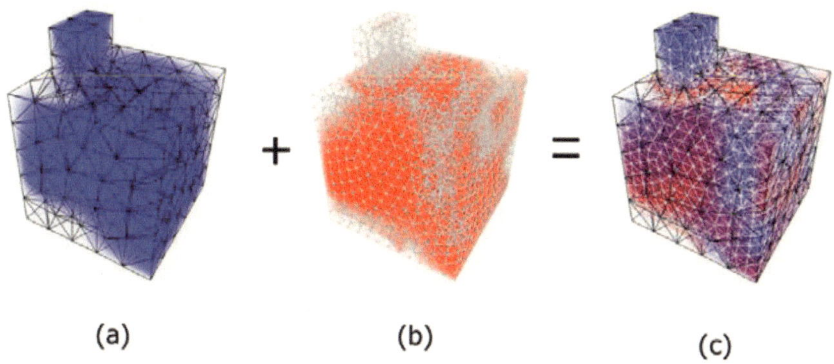

Figure 4.
Example of application to "Tank" data. (a) Velocity data defined by 516 cells, (b) pressure data defined by 9827 cells, (c) (a)+(b) fused visualization.

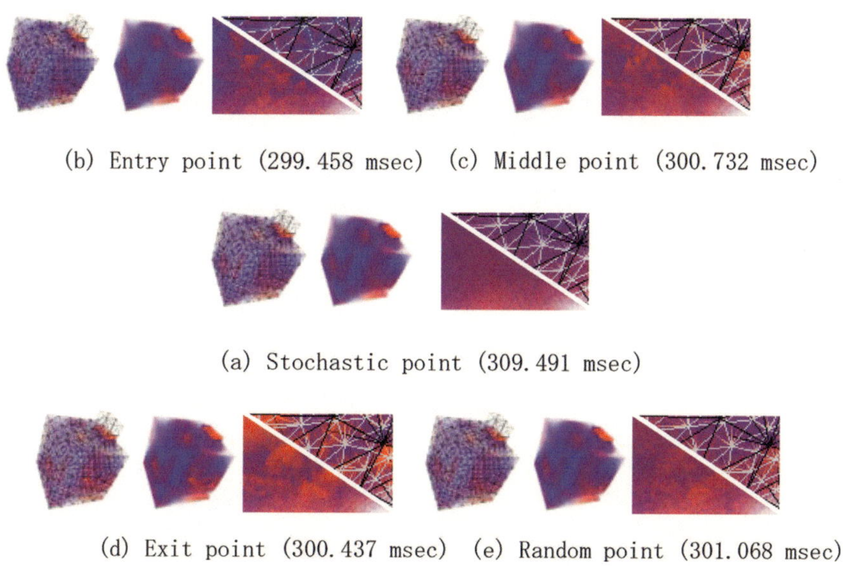

Figure 5.
Comparison of application example to "Tank" data by the proposed method and conventional methods.

absence), the time required for the visualization result is described. Obviously, with the conventional method, it can be understood that artifacts due to improper setting of the depth value are visible in the visualization results. In particular, the trend is noticeable in the visualization results (b–d) where the depth value is set at the fixed point of the section. Even with the random position, it is more noticeable than that of the proposed method (e). Additionally, it can be seen that there is almost no difference in the calculation time required for the visualization.

6. Conclusion

In this chapter, we proposed a volume rendering algorithm method for multiple irregular volume data. In this method, the tetrahedral grid constituting the volume data is projected on the image plane, and the opacity is used to control the presence/absence of drawing at pixel expansion. To efficiently perform volume rendering of multiple irregular volume data, we developed a method for stochastically arranging particles in the section where the viewing ray is cut off by tetrahedrons. In this arrangement method, the particle position is calculated by inverse function method, considering the particle position as a random variable and the cumulative distribution function as opacity.

In the experiments for confirming the effectiveness of this method, we prepared two types of irregular volume data with different cells and confirmed the effectiveness of the proposed method in terms of the presence/absence of artifacts and calculation time at the intersection of the cells.

Although this time we concerned the proposal of the visualization method itself, we would like to use this method to elucidate the causal relationship between variables in important physical phenomena. For example, in order to clarify the influence of coherent vortices on heat transport in thermal fluid phenomena, it is necessary to combine scalar data representing a second invariant representing a vortex region and scalar data representing a heat flux absolute value related to heat transport. By using this method for the visualization of two kinds of time series irregular volume data, we would like to figure out a visual correlation between the multiple variables.

Author details

Koji Koyamada[1*] and Naohisa Sakamoto[2]

1 Kyoto University, Kyoto, Japan

2 Kobe University, Kobe, Japan

*Address all correspondence to: koyamada.koji.3w@kyoto-u.ac.jp

References

[1] Sakamoto N, Nonaka J, Koyamada K, Tanaka S. Particle-based volume rendering. In: Proceedings of Asia-Pacific Symposium on Visualization (APVIS 2007); 2007. pp. 129-132

[2] Sakamoto N, Kawamura T, Koyamada K. Improvement of particle-based volume rendering for visualizing irregular volume data sets. Computers & Graphics. 2010;**34**(1):34-42

[3] Sakamoto N, Kawamura T, Kuwano H, Koyamada K. Sorting-free pre-intergrated projected tetrahedra. In: Proceedings of the 2009 Workshop on Ultrascale Visualization 2009; 2009. pp. 11-18

[4] Blinn J. Light reflection function for simulation of clouds and dusty surfaces. Computers and Graphics. 1982;**16**(3): 21-29

[5] Sabella P. A rendering algorithm for visualizing 3D scalar field. Computers and Graphics. 1988;**22**(4):51-58

[6] Drebin RA, Carpenter L, Hanrahan P. Volume rendering. Computers and Graphics. 1988;**22**(4):65-74

[7] Levoy M. Display of surfaces from volume data. IEEE Computer Graphics and Applications. 1988;**8**(3):29-37

[8] Hansen C, Johnson C. The Visualization Handbook. Elsevier; 2005

[9] Silva C, Comba J, Callahan S, Bernardon F. A survey of GPU-based volume rendering on unstructured grids. Brazillian Journal of Theoretic and Applied Computing. 2005;**12**(2):9-29

[10] Lu Cai, Yuan Mingkai, Wang Qi, Kang Kun. Application of multi-attributes fused volume rendering techniques in 3D seismic interpretation. 2014:1609–1613

[11] Engel K, Kraus M, Ertl T. High-quality pre-integrated volume rendering using hardware-accelerated pixel shading. In: Proc. of Eurographics/ SIGGRAPH Workshop on Graphics Hardware; 2001. pp. 9-16

[12] Sakamoto N, Koyamada K. Stoachastic approach for integrated rendering of volumes and semi-transparent surfaces. In: Proceedings of the 2012 Workshop on Ultrascale Visualization 2012; 2012

[13] Meredith J, Ma KL. Multiresolution view-dependent splat-based volume rendering of large irregular data. In: Proc. IEEE 2001 Symp. on Parallel and Large-Data Visualization and Graphics; 2001. pp. 93-155

[14] Westover L. Footprint evaluation for volume rendering. Computers and Graphics. 1990;**24**(4):367-376

Chapter 6

Design and Implementation of Particle Systems for Meshfree Methods with High Performance

Giuseppe Bilotta, Vito Zago and Alexis Hérault

Abstract

Particle systems, commonly associated with computer graphics, animation, and video games, are an essential component in the implementation of numerical methods ranging from the meshfree methods for computational fluid dynamics and related applications (e.g., smoothed particle hydrodynamics, SPH) to minimization methods for arbitrary problems (e.g., particle swarm optimization, PSO). These methods are frequently embarrassingly parallel in nature, making them a natural fit for implementation on massively parallel computational hardware such as modern graphics processing units (GPUs). However, naive implementations fail to fully exploit the capabilities of this hardware. We present practical solutions to the challenges faced in the efficient parallel implementation of these particle systems, with a focus on performance, robustness, and flexibility. The techniques are illustrated through GPUSPH, the first implementation of SPH to run completely on GPU, and currently supporting multi-GPU clusters, uniform precision independent of domain size, and multiple SPH formulations.

Keywords: software design, particle systems, SPH, GPGPU, high-performance computing, numerical stability, best practices

1. Introduction

Particle systems were first formally introduced in computer science by Reeves [1], as the technique used by Lucasfilm Ltd. for the realization of some of the special effects present in the film *Star Trek II: The Wrath of Khan* [2]. Since then, particle systems have been used in computer graphics for the simulation of visually realistic fire, moving water, clouds, dust, lava, and snow. A particle system consists of a collection of distinct elements (particles) that are generated according to specific rules, evolve and move in the simulation space, and die out at the end of their life cycle. The position and characteristics of the particles in the system over simulated time are then used to render larger bodies (flames, rivers, etc.) with appropriate techniques [3].

While originally developed purely for visual effects, and associated with evolution laws focused on the final appearance rather than the physical correctness of the behavior, particle systems also form the digital infrastructure for the implementation of a class of numerical methods (known as meshless, meshfree, or particle methods) that have started emerging since the late 1970s as alternatives to the traditional grid-based numerical methods (finite differences, finite volumes, finite elements). These methods—smoothed particle hydrodynamics (SPH) [4], reproducing kernel particle method (RKPM) [5], finite pointset method (FPM) [6], discrete element method (DEM) [7], etc.—provide rigorous methods to discretize the physical laws governing the continuum and thus provide physics-based evolution law for the properties of the particles that act both as interpolation nodes in the mathematical sense and as virtual volumes of infinitesimal size carrying the properties of the macroscopic mass they represent.

More recently, the same computer techniques have been used to solve more abstract problems. For example, particle swarm optimization (PSO) [8] is a methodology to find approximate minima for functions whose derivatives cannot be computed (at all or in reasonable times), in spaces of arbitrary dimensions. Outside of the particle systems in the proper sense, simulation methods such as molecular dynamics (MD) [9] and many large-scale agent-based models present significant similarities with particle systems [10, 11] and share much of the infrastructural work with it.

Particle systems are computationally intensive. Realistic visual effects, accurate physical simulations, fast minimization, and large-scale agent-based models all require thousands if not millions (or more) of particles. On the upside, the behavior of most particle systems can be described in an embarrassingly parallel way, where each particle evolves either independently from the rest of the system or with at most local knowledge of the state of the system. This property makes particle systems a perfect fit for implementation on massively parallel computational hardware following the stream processing programming model, and in particular modern graphics processing units (GPUs), that have grown in the last decade from fast, programmable 3D rendering hardware to more general-purpose computing accelerators [12].

While the parallel computational power of GPUs is a natural fit for the parallel nature of particle systems, naive implementations will miss many opportunities to fully exploit GPUs, even when achieving performance orders of magnitude higher than an unoptimized, serial CPU implementation. Our objective is to discuss the optimal implementation of particle systems on GPU, so that anyone setting forth to implement a particle system can draw from our experience to avoid common pitfalls and be aware of the implications of many design choices. Optimality will be viewed in terms of performance (achieving the highest number of iterations per second in the evolution of the system), robustness (numerical stability), and flexibility (allowing the implementation of a wide range of variants for the particle system, e.g., to allow the simulation of different phenomena).

We will show that while these objectives are sometimes in conflict—so that the developer will have to choose to, e.g., sacrifice performance for better numerical stability—there are also cases where they complement each other, e.g., with some numerically more robust approaches also being more computationally efficient or with certain design choices for the host code structure being also more favorable to future extensions to multi-GPU support.

We will make extensive reference to our experience from the implementation of GPUSPH [13–17], the first implementation of SPH to run completely on GPU using CUDA and currently supporting multi-GPU and multi-node distribution of the computation. However, all the themes that we discuss and solutions we present are of interest to all particle systems and related methods, regardless of the specific theoretical background underlying them. To show this, simpler examples to illustrate the benefits of individual topics discussed will also be presented through a reduced implementation of PSO. Some of the most advanced techniques described can be seen in action in GPUSPH itself, which is freely available under the GNU General Public License, version 3 or higher [18].

While our focus will be on GPU implementation, many of the approaches we discuss can bring significant benefits even on CPU implementations, allowing better exploitation of the vector hardware and multiple cores of current hardware. The intention is thus to provide material that is of practical use regardless of the specific application and hardware.

2. Terminology and notation

Throughout the paper, we will rely on the terminology used by the cross-platform OpenCL standard [19]. All the concepts we discuss will be equally valid in different programming contexts, such as the proprietary CUDA developed by NVIDIA specifically for their GPU and HPC solutions [20]. This choice stems from the authors' opinion that the OpenCL terminology is more neutral and less susceptible to the kind of confusion that some vendors have leveraged as a marketing tactic in promoting their solutions.

In our examples, we will also frequently refer to "small vector" data types. These are types in the form `typeN` where `type` is a primitive type (such as `char`, `int`, `float`, `double`) and `N` is one of 1, 2, 3, 4, 8, and 16. For example, a `float4` would be a structure that in C or C++ could be defined as `struct float4 {float x, y, z, w;}`. Following OpenCL, the components of the small vector types will be named `x`, `y`, `z`, `w` for types with up to 4 components, and `s0`, ... `s9`, `sa`, ... `sf` for types with up to 16 components. In some examples we also make use of the OpenCL "swizzle notation," such that, for example, given `float2 v=(0.0f, 1.0f);`, then `v.xxyy` is a `float4` with components `(0.0f, 0.0f, 1.0f, 1.0f)`.

We will assume that each small vector type is "naturally aligned," when `N` is a power of two: a `typeN` will begin at a memory address which is a multiple of `N*sizeof(type)`; for `N=3`, we will assume that `type3` begins at a memory address which is a multiple of `sizeof(type)`. This is in contrast to OpenCL, whose `cl_type3` types are assumed to be aligned like the corresponding `cl_type4` types, and special `vload3` instructions are needed to load packed 3-vectors. We will also show momentarily that such 3-component types should in general be avoided as they lead to lower performance, since most if not all modern hardware are designed around power-of-two types (which is the reason why the OpenCL type is aligned to four components).

Finally, we will assume that the standard operations (component-by-component addition, subtraction, and multiplication, multiplication by a scalar, dot product) on the small vector types have been defined, in the usual manner. (OpenCL C defines these as part of the language, for CUDA appropriate overloads for the common operators must be defined by the user.)

3. The GPU programming model

3.1 Stream processing

Modern GPUs are designed around the *stream processing* paradigm, a simplified model for shared-memory parallel programming that sacrifices inter-unit communication in favor of higher efficiency and scalability.

At an abstract level, stream processing is defined by a sequence of instructions (a *computational kernel*) to be executed on each element of an input data stream to produce an output data stream, under the assumption that each input element can be processed independently from the others (and thus in parallel). A computational kernel is similar to a standard function in classic imperative programming languages; at runtime, as many instances of the function will be executed as necessary to cover the whole input data stream. Such instances (*work-items*) may be dispatched in concurrent batches, running in parallel as far as the hardware allows, and the programmer is generally given very little control, if any, on the dispatch itself, other than being able to specify how many instances are needed in total. This choice allows the same kernel to be executed on the same data stream, adapting naturally to the characteristics of the underlying hardware, and is one of the main characteristics of stream processing.

For example, if the hardware can run 1000 concurrent work-items, but the input stream consists of 2000,000 total elements, the hardware may batch 1000 work-items for execution at once and then dispatch another 1000 when the first batch completes execution. This continues until the entire input stream has been processed, executing 2000 total batches. For the same workloads, more powerful hardware able to run 100,000 concurrent work-items may be able to complete sooner by issuing 20 total batches, in a manner completely transparent to the programmer.

This programming model fits very well the simpler workload needed in many steps of the rendering process for which GPUs are designed: in such a case, the input and output streams may consist of the data and attributes for the vertices in the geometries describing the scene, for example, or for the fragments produced by the rasterization of such geometries. However, the more sophisticated requirements of general-purpose programming have led to the extension of the stream processing paradigm to provide programmers with finer control on the work-item dispatch as well as the possibility for efficient data sharing between work-items under appropriate conditions.

A modern stream processing *device* (typically a GPU, but may also be a multicore CPU with vector units, a dedicated accelerator like Intel's Xeon Phi, or a special-design FPGA) is composed of one or more *compute unit*s (each being a CPU core, a GPU multiprocessor, etc.) equipped with one or more *processing elements* (a SIMD lane on CPU, a single stream processor on GPU, etc.), which are the hardware components that process the individual work-items during a kernel execution. The programming model of these devices, as presented, e.g., by standards such as OpenCL [19] and by proprietary solutions such as NVIDIA CUDA [20], exposes the underlying hardware structure by allowing the programmer to specify the granularity at which work-items should be dispatched: each *workgroup* is a collection of work-items that are guaranteed to run on a single compute unit; work-items within the same workgroup can share data efficiently through dedicated (often on-chip) memory and can synchronize with each other, ensuring correct instruction ordering. Tuning workgroup size and the way work-items in the same workgroup access data can have a significant impact on performance.

The GPU multiprocessors are further characterized by an additional level of work-item grouping at the hardware level, as the work-items running on a single multiprocessor are not independent from each other: instead, a single instruction pointer is shared by a fixed-width group of work-items, known as the *warp* on NVIDIA GPUs, or *wavefront* on AMD GPUs, corresponding in a very general sense to the vector width of SIMD instructions on modern CPUs. We will use the hardware-independent term *subgroup* (as introduced, e.g., in OpenCL 2.0) to denote this hardware grouping. The subgroup structure of kernel execution influences performance in a number of ways. The most obvious way is that the size of a workgroup should always be a multiple of the subgroup size: a partial subgroup would be fully dispatched anyway, but masked, leading to lower hardware usage. Additional aspects where the subgroup partitioning can influence performance are branch divergence and coalesced memory access.

Branch divergence occurs when work-items belonging to the same subgroup need to take different execution paths at a given conditional. Since the subgroup proceeds in lockstep for all intents and purposes, in such a situation the hardware must mask the work-items not satisfying either branch, execute one side of the branch, invert the mask, and execute the other side of the branch: the total runtime cost is then the sum of the runtimes of each branch. If the work-items taking different execution paths belong to separate subgroups, this cost is not incurred, because separate subgroups can execute concurrently on different code paths, leading to an overall runtime cost equal to that of the longer branch.

Coalescence in memory access is achieved when the controller of a GPU can provide data for the entire subgroup with a single memory transaction. Ensuring that this happens is one of the primary aspects of efficient GPU implementations and will be the basis for many of the performance hints discussed later on.

3.2 Stream processing and particle systems

Stream processing is a natural fit for the implementation of particle systems, since the vast majority of algorithms that rely on particle systems are embarrassingly parallel in nature, with the behavior of each particle determined independently, thus providing a natural map between particles and work-items for most kernels. This allows naive implementations of particle systems to be developed very quickly, often with massive performance gains over trivial serial implementations running on single-core CPUs.

Such implementations will however generally fail at leveraging the full computational power of GPUs, except in the simplest of cases. Any moderately sophisticated algorithm will frequently require a violation of the natural mapping of particles to stream elements (and thus work-items), either in terms of data structure and access or in terms of implementation logic, to be able to achieve the optimal performance on any given hardware.

3.3 Limitations in the use of GPUs

Programmable GPUs have brought forth a revolution in computing, making (certain forms of) large-scale parallel computing accessible to the masses. Many applications have seen significant benefit from a transition to the GPU as supporting hardware, and in response vendors have improved GPU architectures, making it easier to achieve better performance with less implementation effort.

When choosing the GPU as preferential target platform, however, developers must take into consideration the fact that not all users may have high-end professional GPUs, and while the stream computing paradigm is largely sufficient in compensating for the difference in computational power, there are at least two significant aspects that must be explicitly handled.

Memory amount is one of these issues: consumer GPUs typically only have a fraction of the total amount of RAM offered in professional or compute-dedicated devices: while the latter may feature up to 16GB of RAM, low-end devices may have 1/4th or even 1/8th of that. Moreover, even the amount of memory available on high-end devices may be insufficient to handle larger problems. Software should therefore be designed to allow distribution of computation across multiple devices.

The second issue is that, being designed for computer graphics, GPUs typically focus on single-precision (32-bit) floating-point operations, and double precision (64-bit) may be either not supported at all or supported at a much lower execution rate (as low as 1:32) than single precision, which may remove the computational advantage of using GPUs in the first place (this can be true even on high-end GPUs, as was infamously the case for the Maxwell-class Tesla GPUs from NVIDIA). Designing the software around the use of single precision can therefore allow supporting higher performance across a wider class of devices, but it may require particular care in the handling of essential state variables in particle systems. This will be discussed in Section 5.

4. Performance

While GPUs provide impressive computational power compared to CPUs, this is offset by a much higher sensitivity to data layout and access patterns: even a very computationally intensive kernel may result memory bound if the appropriate care is not given to these aspects.

The main GPU memory (*global* memory) is characterized by having high bandwidth, but also very high latency: access to global memory may consume hundreds of cycles, and work-items waiting for data will not proceed until the data is available to all of them, at least at the subgroup granularity.

Under appropriate conditions (called memory coalescing or fast-path), the GPU can provide data for a whole subgroup with a single memory transaction. Optimal access patterns in this regard are achieved when the work-items in a subgroup request data which is consecutive in memory, properly aligned (i.e., with the lowest-index element starting at an address which is a multiple of the data size times the subgroup size), and with specific size constraints—typically power-of-two sizes, up to 128 bits per work-item: essentially, the equivalent of a `float`, `float2`, or `float4`, but not `float3`.

When fast-path requirements are not satisfied, the impact on kernel run times can be dramatic, especially on older architectures: designing data structures and algorithms around these requirements is therefore one of the main topics we will address. But even when coalesced access is achieved, each subgroup will have to wait for at least one memory transaction before proceeding to the instruction that makes use of the data. To hide this latency, GPU multiprocessors are designed to keep multiple workgroups alive concurrently and will automatically switch to another active workgroup (or subgroup within the same workgroup), while one is stalled waiting for data; to make efficient use of this capability, it is necessary to *overcommit* the device, i.e., issue kernels with more workgroups than would theoretically be able to run concurrently on the given hardware.

For example, on a GPU with 16 multiprocessors, each equipped with 128 streaming processors, it will not be sufficient to issue kernels with 2048 work-items to fully exploit the hardware: to fully hide operation latency, the developer should aim for global work sizes which are at least an order of magnitude more than the bare minimum.

A GPU that is fully under load is said to be *saturated*. On most modern architectures, tens of thousands of work-items are generally necessary to saturate mid- and high-end devices. This condition is usually satisfied for any moderate or large particle system, in which case the data layout and access patterns become the bottleneck for memory bandwidth utilization.

4.1 Array of structures versus structure of array

The first step in improving GPU bandwidth usage is to avoid high-level structured data layouts and store information about the particle system in a "transposed" format.

Let us consider, for example, a simple particle system in three dimensions, where each particle is described by its position (3 floats) and velocity (3 floats). In a CPU implementation, data would be stored in a format based on a `Particle` structure, and the particle system would be an array of `Particles`. Integrating the particles' position over a time-step `dt` would be achieved in a simple loop like the one illustrated in **Listing 1**.

This approach is called *array of structures* (AoS), and assuming a stream processing perspective, preserving the same layout would lead to a compute kernel in the form presented on the left in **Listing 2**. However, since each particle is more than 128 bit wide, the GPU would not be able to satisfy each subgroup access to the `particle_system` (marked by the comments) in a single transaction, resulting in a potential slowdown of an order of magnitude or more. A better solution on GPU would be to split the particle structure in each primary component and thus have, in this case, an array of positions and an array of velocities, as shown on the right in **Listing 2**.

Part of the advantage of this approach (*structure of arrays*, SoA) is the natural higher access granularity, which limits read and write access to what is strictly necessary. With the AoS approach, it is also possible to limit writes to the specific parts, e.g., `particle_system[i].pos+= particle_system[i].vel*dt`, but we will see that this only partially recovers the performance gap against SoA. Moreover, the access granularity of SoA also reflects in the function signatures, improving developer discipline. The downside is the growing number of buffers, and strategies to manage this will be discussed in Section 6.2.1.

Listing 1.
Simple host code to integrate the position of a particle system.

```
struct Particle {
    float3 pos;
    float3 vel;
};
```

```
void
integrate_pos(Particle *particle_system,
    size_t N, float dt)
{
    for (size_t i=0; i<num_particles; ++i) {
        Particle& p=particle_system[i];
        p.pos+= p.vel*dt;
    }
}
```

Listing 2.
Particle system with stream processing: array of structure (left) versus structure of array (right).

```
kernel void
integrate_pos(Particle *particle_system,
    size_t N, float dt)
{
    size_t i=get_global_id(0);
    if (i>= N) return;
    /* read the old particle state */
    Particle p=particle_system[i];
    p.pos+= p.vel*dt;
    /* write the new particle state */
    particle_system[i]=p;
}
```

```
kernel void
integrate_pos(float3 *posArray,
    const float3 *velArray,
    size_t N, float dt)
{
    size_t i=get_global_id(0);
    if (i>= N) return;
    float3 pos=posArray[i];
    const float3 vel=velArray[i];
    pos+= vel*dt;
    posArray[i]=pos;
}
```

Further optimizations, particularly important on older architectures, can be achieved with the sacrifice of some memory, to provide the position and velocity with a fourth (unused) component, as illustrated in **Listing 3** (left), resulting in better bandwidth usage and thus faster execution; moreover, additional frequently used data may be stored in the fourth component, if needed (e.g., in GPUSPH we store the mass in pos.w and the density in vel.w).

The benefits of the discussed strategies are exemplified in **Table 1** for a simple three-dimensional implementation of PSO. The specific values will obviously generally depend on the specific compute kernel as well as on the specific hardware.

Some additional (usually minor) benefits can be achieved by explicitly telling the compiler that the position and velocity array never intersect; this is achieved using the `restrict` specification for the pointer (**Listing 3**, right) which, for more complex kernels, may allow the compiler to produce faster code by assuming no dependencies between writes on one array and reads on the other. On some hardware, `const * restrict` arrays are also made accessible through a dedicated cache, further improving performance.

4.2 Wide arrays

The SoA approach can provide a significant boost in performance on GPU, as long as the individual parts of the structure (position, velocity, etc.) fit within the size requirements for coalesced memory access. When even individual structure members are wider than the optimal 128-bit width, however, alternative approaches are necessary. An example of this occurrence is the storage of a list of

Listing 3.
Using efficient data types on GPU (left) and leveraging the power of restricted pointers (right).

```
kernel void
integrate_pos(float4 *posArray,
      const float4 *velArray,
      size_t N, float dt)
{
      size_t i=get_global_id(0);
      if (i>= N) return;
      float4 pos=posArray[i];
      const float4 vel=velArray[i];
      pos.xyz+= vel.xyz*dt; /* OpenCL swizzle */
      posArray[i]=pos;
}
```

```
kernel void
integrate_pos(float4 * restrict posArray,
      const float4 * restrict velArray,
      size_t N, float dt)
{
      size_t i=get_global_id(0);
      if (i>= N) return;
      float4 pos=posArray[i];
      const float4 vel=velArray[i];
      pos.xyz+= vel.xyz*dt; /* OpenCL swizzle */
      posArray[i]=pos;
}
```

	AoS	Selective AoS	SoA	Padded SoA
Runtime (ms)	98	73	25	13
Speedup (prev)	—	1.3	2.9	1.9
Speedup (total)	—	1.3	3.9	7.5

2^24 particles running on an NVIDIA GeForce GT 750M.

Table 1.
Runtime comparison for a simple three-dimensional particle swarm optimization implementation, using the discussed paradigms: array of structures, array of structures with selective writing, structure of arrays, structure of arrays with padded members (i.e., using four instead of three components).

neighbors; frequently, the number of neighbors for a particle will range in the tens or hundreds, sometimes even more, requiring storage of as many integers per particle. Another example is given by particle systems with high dimensionality (higher than 4), which could arise, for example, for a particle swarm optimization approach to the minimization of the cost function of a deep neural network. The position (and velocities) of particles in such a system might require hundreds, thousands, or even more, components.

The optimal storage solution for the array holding the data in such cases is transposed compared to the natural order: whereas for most CPU code it is natural to first store the data belonging to the first particle, then the data belonging to the second particle, etc., the optimal GPU storage for these wide arrays is to first store the first component for each particle, followed by the second component for each particle, etc. Using the standard C array notation, the i-th component of the p-th particle in the classic format would be found at location `data[p*num_components+i]`, whereas the optimal GPU location would use the addressing `data [i*num_particles+p]`. Similarly, neighbors would be stored interleaved: the first neighbor of each particle, followed by the second neighbor for each particle, etc. This ensures that when particles iterate over their neighbors, they fetch the neighbor index in coalescence. The concept is illustrated in **Figure 1** (top and middle graphs).

The data transposition can rely on different chunk sizes; the single components approach discussed so far has the benefit of being simpler and the natural choice when each component needs to be treated independently (e.g., neighbors list traversal); if possible, however, wider chunks (e.g., using arrays of `float2` or `float4` elements instead of `float`) should be used (**Figure 1**, bottom), to achieve better utilization of the memory bandwidth.

In general, the balance between transposition and chunk width should be calibrated based on the hardware capability: current GPUs achieve optimal performance with `float4`s, while on a CPU or a Xeon Phi, the wide vector width offered by AVX and AVX-512 could be better exploited using `float8` or `float16` chunks, as illustrated in **Table 2**.

4.3 Particle sorting and neighbor search

In many particle systems, the behavior of the individual particles depends on the state of the particles in a neighborhood of the particle itself. The neighborhood may

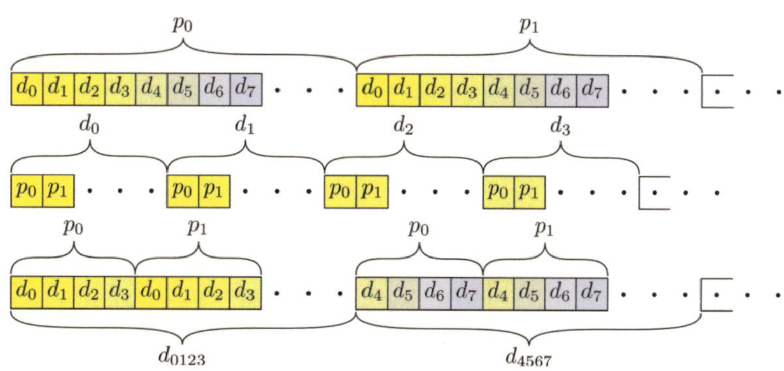

Figure 1.
Possible memory layouts for wide arrays. Top, standard (particle-major) layout; middle, transposed (component-major) layout; bottom, transpose-chunked layout. Memory locations are colored by data component access: locations with the same color are accessed concurrently in parallel by all work-items. In the chunked case, more than one location may be accessed concurrently, depending on the chunk size and hardware capability.

Hardware	Naïve	Transposed	Chunk 2	Chunk 4	Chunk 8	Chunk 16
NVIDIA	476	41	39	***38***	48	71
Intel GPU	237	75	63	***58***	59	91
Intel CPU	120	568	294	422	53	***41***

The NVIDIA GPU is a GeForce GT 750M; the Intel GPU is an Intel HD Graphics Haswell GT2 Mobile, using the Beignet OpenCL implementation from Intel; the Intel CPU is an Intel Core i7-4712HQ, using the Intel OpenCL SDK 6.4.0.25. Bold italic values show the best performance. The CPU exhibits worse performance for the transposed layout than the naive due to the auto-vectorization introduced by the OpenCL implementation.

Table 2.
Median runtimes (in ms) of the position update kernel for a 128-dimensional particle swarm optimization using the described memory layouts, on different hardware.

be defined in terms of some fixed influence radius or may be determined dynamically, either based on a changing influence radius or based on a pure neighbors count (e.g., "the 10 closest neighbors"). Performance of particle systems on GPU can be improved by reordering particle data in memory so that the data for particles that are close to each other in the domain metric (e.g., distance) are also close in device memory, providing more opportunities for coalesced memory access and (when available) better cache utilization [21].

Sorting is generally achieved using key/value pairs, with the particle hash key computed from the particle position in space: the key array is then sorted, and all data arrays are reordered based on the new key array positions. Common ways to compute the particle sort key are based on either n-trees [22] or regular grids [23]. The main advantage of using an n-tree (and thus in particular quadtrees in 2D and octrees in 3D) is the adaptive nature of the structure, which is denser where particles are concentrated and sparser in the domain regions where particles are more spread out. By contrast, regular grids result in cells which are uniformly spaced and thus in unbalanced particle distributions among the cells.

The adaptive nature of n-trees can result in performance gains in a number of use cases, such as nearest-neighbor searches, collision detection, clump finding, and rendering. At the same time, traversing the tree structure itself efficiently on a stream processing architecture is nontrivial and often results in sub-optimal memory bandwidth utilization [24]. Regular grids, on the other hand, have a much simpler and computationally less expensive implementation, they lead to efficient neighbor search with fixed radius (as we will discuss momentarily), and the resulting data structures can also be used to support domain decomposition in the multi-GPU case, as we will discuss in Section 4.5.3, and also to improve the numerical robustness of the particle system, as we will discuss in Section 5.4.

4.3.1 Regular grids for neighbor search

Given a neighbor search radius r, we can subdivide the domain with a regular grid where the stepping in each direction is no less than r. This guarantees that the neighbors for any particle in any given cell can only be found at most in the adjacent cells in each of the cardinal and diagonal directions (Moore neighborhood of radius 1), as depicted in **Figure 2**.

We can then sort particles (i.e., their data) by, e.g., the linear index or the Morton code [25] of the cell they belong to (computed from the particle global position), so that data for all particles belonging to one cell ends up in a consecutive memory region. Furthermore, we can store in a separate array the offset (common

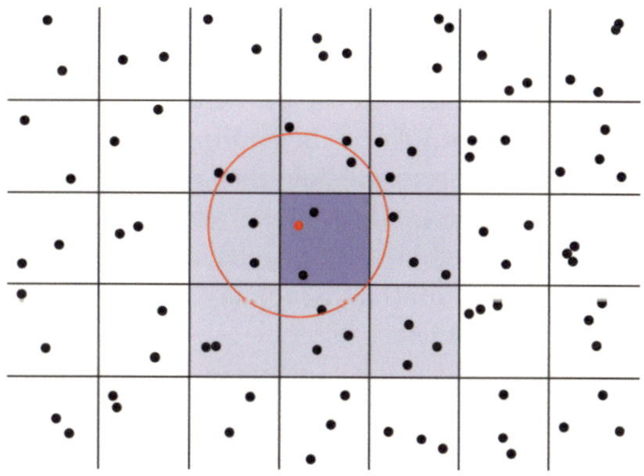

Figure 2.
Support grid for neighbor search: if the cell side is no less than the influence radius, the neighbors for any particle in any given cell (dark blue square in the picture) can be found in at most the Moore neighborhood of the cell itself (light blue squares in the picture).

to all data arrays) to the beginning of the data for the particles in each cell (**Figure 3**).

A single particle can then search for neighbors by only looking at the corresponding subsets of the particle system, starting from the cell start index for each adjacent cell. Since all particles belonging in the same cell will need to traverse the same subset of the particle list, further improvements can be obtained by loading the data about the potential neighbors into a shared-memory array.

4.3.2 Just-in-time neighbor search versus neighbor list storage

The results of the neighbor search may be used immediately (e.g., by computing the particle-particle interaction as each neighbor is found) or deferred: in the latter case, the neighbor search itself constitutes its own step in the system evolution, and the results of the search are stored in a list which is then used in subsequent kernels when particle-particle interactions must be computed.

The "just-in-time" approach (which can be equivalently seen as searching for neighbors whenever needed) has the advantage of lower memory requirements (since the list of neighbors needs not be stored), but the disadvantage that the cost of the search itself must be paid whenever interactions must be computed. Therefore, it is the preferred approach when the results of each search are only needed once. Conversely, when the results of the neighbor search are to be used multiple times, it is better, performance-wise, to store the results, and then reuse them in the

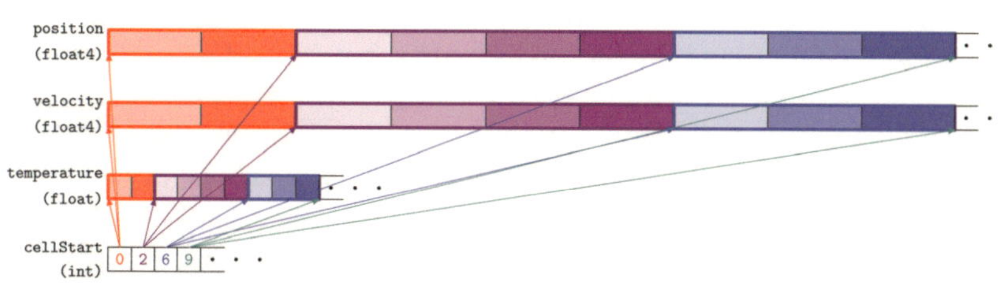

Figure 3.
Memory layout for the support grid. Data arrays are sorted so that the data belonging to particles in any given cell is consecutive in memory, and a separate array holds the offset to the beginning of the data of the particles in each cell. In the picture, each primary color denotes a cell, and the color gradient refers to different particle data within each cell. The first cell has two particles, the second has four particles, and the third has three.

following steps, in order to amortize the cost of the search. The downside in this case is much higher memory requirements.

For example, in GPUSPH the cost of the particle sorting and neighbor list construction can take as much as 30% of the runtime of a single step; most of this (25% of the step runtime) is spent in the neighbor search phase of the neighbor list construction; the list itself is then used for all subsequent kernels that require particle-particle interaction (boundary conditions, density smoothing, forces computation, surface detection, etc., most of which are executed twice due to the predictor/corrector integration scheme used).

Working without a neighbor list, the runtime cost of the search would have to be paid for each execution of a kernel with particle-particle interaction, increasing the runtime of a single operation by over 50%. The neighbor list is therefore a better choice for performance.

On the other hand, on a typical simulation in GPUSPH, the neighbor list is also responsible for the highest memory allocation, even including the double buffering required for most data arrays: indeed, all of the particle properties combined take between 100 and 300 bytes per particle (depending on the formulation being used), whereas for the neighbor list, we need to store, in the simplest cases, 128 neighbors, leading to an occupation of 512 bytes per particle. Some formulations may require two or three times as many neighbors per particle.

We remark that even when not all particles have the exact same number of neighbors, the neighbor list should be statically allocated at the beginning of the simulation, with the capacity to hold the maximum (expected) number of neighbors for any particle and with the layout discussed in Section 4.2, to maximize the performance of its traversal. This leads to some potential memory waste for the benefit of performance. However, even a more conservative and less wasteful neighbor list would still occupy significant memory (e.g., a median of 80 neighbors per particle still needs to be tracked on a typical GPUSPH simulation, which only lowers the memory occupation for the neighbor list to 320 bytes per particle). The net result is that the large allocations required by the neighbor list will limit the maximum size of a particle system that can be simulated on a single GPU.

Additionally, even with the stored neighbor list, nearly one-third of a simulation step is still taken by its construction. A solution to this issue is to only update the list every n iterations, with n large enough to reduce the performance impact and small enough to not affect the results in a significant way. With the default choice of $n = 10$ in GPUSPH, the cost of particle sorting and neighbor search drops to around 5% of the total runtime in the worst cases. To improve the reliability of the simulations when neighbor list updates are less frequent, a good strategy is to increase the search radius: with this approach, given an influence radius r (maximum distance for interaction), the neighbors are actually added to the list of neighbors if their distance from the central particle is less than αr, with $\alpha>1$; neighbors whose distance from the central particle is larger than r are then skipped in the kernels. The larger search radius takes into account the fact that particles may move before the next neighbor list update, thus bringing them closer. In this sense, the expansion factor for the neighbor search should be computed based on $nv_M\Delta t$, where v_M is the maximum expected (relative) particle velocity and Δt the maximum expected time step.

4.4 Heterogeneous particle systems

While simple particle systems are often homogeneous (in that all particles behave the same way), many applications require heterogeneous particle systems, where particles behave differently depending on some intrinsic characteristic. For example, SPH for fluid dynamics typically needs at least two different particle types: fluid particles that track the fluid itself and boundary particles that define solid walls, moving objects, etc.; the way particles interact with each other (or even whether or not they interact at all) in this case depends on both the central and neighboring particle type.

Heterogeneity in the behavior of the particles and their interactions can have a significant impact on the performance of the system, particularly when it is stored together, without any specific attention to the distribution of the particles and their types. Indeed, the natural way to process a particle system is to issue, for most kernels, a work-item per particle. However, when particles with different types or behavior are processed by work-items in the same subgroup, this leads to divergence, slowing down execution. Similarly, when particles iterate over neighbors, they may have neighbors of different types at corresponding indices (e.g., the third neighbor of the first particle may be a fluid neighbor, while the third neighbor of the second particle might be a boundary neighbor); in this case, again, kernel execution will incur divergences, even if the central particles are of the same type. Moreover, since the distinction between particle types and interaction form must be done at kernel runtime, the kernel code itself grows more complex, reducing optimization opportunities for the compiler and leading to sub-optimal usage of private variables, frequently resulting in register spills, where a reserved area of global memory gets used for temporary storage of private work-item variables, with a severe impact on performance.

When the heterogeneous behavior is due to some static property (e.g., a fixed particle type property), the most obvious choice is to split the particle system itself (e.g., have a particle system for fluid particles and a separate particle system for boundary particles). This has several advantages: it is possible to run a kernel on particles of a specific type more efficiently while still making it possible to run a kernel on all particles; it is also possible to do selective allocations, for example, if a given property (e.g., object number) is only needed for a specific type. The downside is that the management code becomes more complex, and kernels where particles of one type need to interact with particles of the other type must be given access to both sets of arrays, which can increase the complexity of the kernel signatures.

A simpler approach that does not completely solve the divergence issue but can greatly reduce the occurrences of divergence is to introduce additional sorting criteria. For example, one can sort particles by cell, and within cell then sort particles by type, so that for any cell one finds first all the fluid particles (in that cell), followed by all the boundary particles (in the same cell). This "specialized sorting" approach reduces the occurrences of subgroups spanning multiple types to those crossing the boundary between types or between cells. In GPUSPH, the introduction of the per-type sorting within cells has improved the performance of the particle-particle interaction by around 2%. A significant advantage of this approach compared to the split system mentioned before is that it can be used also when the criteria for the behavioral difference are dynamic.

4.4.1 Split neighbor list

Divergence during the neighbor list traversals can be avoided by using a split neighbor list that separately stores neighbors of each type. This comes naturally when using separate particle systems and is efficient also with the specialized sorting approach, since potential neighbors of the same type will be enumerated consecutively in each cell. The split neighbor list can be implemented in such a way that it is possible to iterate efficiently on neighbors of only one given type (or otherwise satisfying one given splitting criterion) while still preserving the possibility to iterate over all neighbors when necessary and minimizing allocation.

A naive split neighbor list can be implemented with separate allocations (e.g., a separate neighbor list per type), but this can quickly lead to an explosion of the already significant memory usage due to the existence of the neighbor list itself: without additional information on the neighbor distribution by type, for example, it may be necessary to allocate a full-sized neighbor list for each type. A more compact solution without loss of traversal efficiency can be achieved by storing the split neighbor list in a single allocation but filling the per-type section of the list from different ends.

As an example, consider the case of two particle types (fluid and boundary), and assume that the neighbor list can hold `M` neighbors per particle (`M` is the maximum number of neighbors any particle can have). For each particle, we store the fluid neighbors starting from position `0` (using the `0`-based indexing common in the C language family), moving forward, and the boundary neighbors starting from position `M-1`, backward, where the indices refer to the particle-specific section of the full neighbor list, and taking interleaving into account as described in Section 4.2; iterating over all fluid neighbors is then achieved in the usual way, whereas iterating over all boundary neighbors would be achieved by traversing the array in reverse, as illustrated in **Listing 4**.

To prevent one section of the neighbor list from bleeding into the other, it is now necessary to put a marker (i.e., an index with a special value, such as −1, defined as `NEIBS_END` in the example in **Listing 4**) at the end of each of the sides of the list, which implies that the effective maximum number of neighbors is reduced by 1 (with the end-of-list marker shared between the two sides when the neighbors list is otherwise full).

If there are more than two types of particle, the same strategy can still be applied, by sectioning the neighbor list. For example, with four types A, B, C, and D, we need to set a value `M1` (the total number of neighbors of type A and B combined) and `M2` (the total number of neighbors of type C and D combined); the neighbor list is allocated to hold `M1+M2` neighbors per particle, where neighbors of type A are stored from position `0` onward, neighbors of type B are stored from position `M1–1` backward, neighbors of type C are stored from position `M1` onward, and neighbors of type D are stored from position `M1+M2–1` backward. Type pairs should be chosen, when possible, based on the uniformity of the cumulative number of neighbors (e.g., if it is more likely that the sum of A and C neighbors is constant, it is better to pair A with C than with B).

Listing 4.
Traversing the split neighbors list: first type (fluid particles in this example) on the left, second type (boundary particle in this example) on the right.

```
int p=get_global_id(0); /* particle index */
for (int i=0; i<M; ++i) {
    /* index of the next fluid neighbor */
    int neib_index=neibsList[i*N+p];
    if (neib_index == NEIBS_END) break;
    /* do stuff with neib_index */
}
```

```
int p=get_global_id(0); /* particle index */
for (int i=M-1; i>=0; --i) {
    /* index of the next boundary neighbor */
    int neib_index=neibsList[i*N+p];
    if (neib_index == NEIBS_END) break;
    /* do stuff with neib_index */
}
```

4.4.2 Split kernels

Once traversal of individual particle types (for the system itself or even just for the neighbors) has been made efficient, the more complex kernels that need to provide significantly different behavior based should be split as well. For example, in GPUSPH we have recently refactored the main computational kernel (dedicated to the computation of the forces acting on each particle) into separate versions to compute fluid/fluid, fluid/boundary, boundary/fluid, etc. interactions. While this generally requires some additional memory access (because, e.g., the particle accelerations now need to be stored and retrieved between one incarnation of the kernel and the next), there has been an overall performance benefit; for the most complex formulations, on first-generation Kepler hardware, we have seen a 50% increase in the number of iterations per second. On the more recent and capable Maxwell architecture, the benefit has been less significant (30% more iterations per second), due to the smaller number of register spills: the more modern hardware supports more registers per work-item and is therefore less affected by the computational issues associated with particle system heterogeneity.

4.5 Multi-GPU

Very large particle systems can benefit from distribution across multiple GPUs. This may in fact be *necessary* simply due to the limited resources available on a single GPU: high-end GPUs currently have at most 16GB of RAM, which may limit the particle system size to a few tens of millions, depending on the complexity of the system. Even for smaller systems, however, distribution over multiple GPUs can provide a performance boost, provided each of the devices is saturated (otherwise, the overhead involved in distributing the particle system will be higher than the benefits offered by the higher computational capacity).

Distributing a particle system across multiple GPUs requires a significant change of vision: GPU coding is facilitated by its shared-memory architecture, where all compute units have read/write access to the entire device global memory. Multi-GPU introduces a distributed parallel computing layer, shifting the focus to efficient work distribution and data exchange between the devices.

For particle systems, the preferential way to distribute work across devices is based on domain decomposition rather than task decomposition, since the former allows both to minimize data exchange and to cover the associated latency more easily. Domain decomposition is achieved by distributing separate sections of the particle system to different devices (e.g., half of the particles and the associated data go on a GPU; the second half goes on a second GPU). When the particles can be processed independently (i.e., no neighborhood information is required), the partition is trivial, and the only objective is load balancing (i.e., ensuring that the fraction of particle system assigned to each GPU is proportional to its computational power). In these cases, the only data exchange needed between GPUs is the tracking of some global quantities, such as the particle system optimal position in PSO.

The decomposition becomes more challenging when the particles' behavior depends on a local neighborhood. In this case, each device must track the state not only of the particles that have been assigned to it but also their neighbors, some of which may have been assigned to other devices. Each device therefore has a view of the particle system as divided in four sections:

- (Strictly) inner particles: particles assigned to the device and that no other device is interested in; no information exchange is involved in their processing.

- Inner edge particles: particles assigned to the device that are neighbors of particles assigned to different devices; information about the evolution of these particles must be sent to other devices.

- Outer edge particles: particles assigned to other devices that are neighbors of particles assigned to this device; information about the evolution of these particles must be received from other devices.

- (Strictly) outer particles: particles assigned to other devices and that this device does not care about; no information exchange is involved in their processing.

The inner/outer relation is symmetrical, in the sense that a (strictly) inner particle for a device is (strictly) outer for all other devices and an inner edge particle for a device is an outer edge particle for at least one other device (**Figure 4**). We will say that two devices are adjacent if they share an inner/outer edge relation (i.e., if they need to exchange data about neighboring particles). Note that, depending on how the particle system is distributed, information about an inner edge particle may need to be sent to multiple adjacent devices.

4.5.1 Computing versus data exchange

The key to an efficient multi-GPU implementation is the ability to minimize the impact of data exchange. The most obvious approach in this sense is to minimize the data transfers themselves, for example, by ensuring that the domain is partitioned in such a way that the number of edge particles is minimized.

As a general rule, during the simulation each device will hold all the data relevant to both its inner (and inner edge) particles and the data relevant to its outer edge particles, i.e., the inner edge particles of adjacent devices. However, it will only run computational kernels on its own particles (using, read-only, the information from the outer edge particles) and then receive updates about the outer edge particles from the adjacent devices. On the other hand, there are cases when it may be convenient for each device to compute the updates for the outer edge particles by

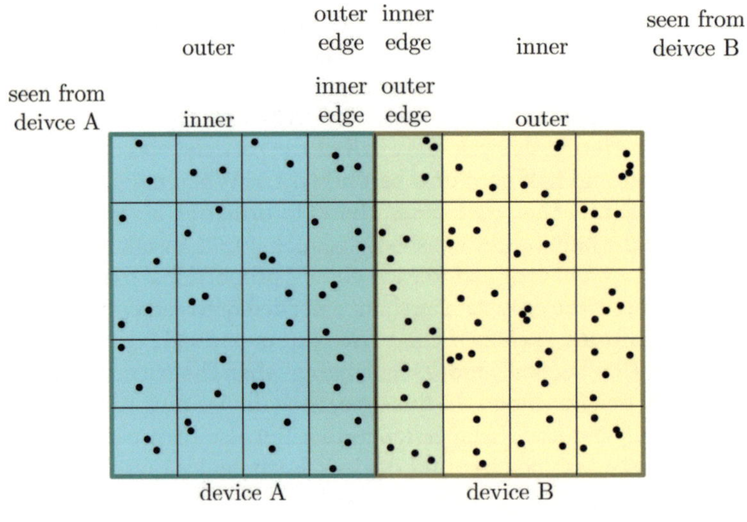

Figure 4.
Inner/outer/edge relationship between devices, with domain decomposition based on a reference grid: inner/outer/edge particles are then defined based on the cell they belong to rather than on a purely geometrical relationship to the particles assigned to other devices.

itself. This can be done under the condition that the update does not require information from the neighbors (since the device does not hold information about all the neighbors of outer edge particles) and becomes convenient when the amount of data to transfer before the update is less than the amount of data to transfer after the update.

As an example, consider a simple particle system where the forces acting on each particle are computed from the interaction with the neighbors (`forces` kernel), but the new position and velocity are computed only from the previously computed forces (`euler` kernel), without any (further) interaction with the neighbors. Assume that there are two devices, D1 and D2, and that all the involved arrays (forces, positions, and velocities) are the same size (e.g., a `float4` per particle). Then it is more convenient for D1 to get the information about the forces acting on its outer edge particles from D2 (and conversely), and then run `euler` on the outer edge particles, than it is for D1 to get the information about the positions and velocities after `euler` has been run on both devices: this is because exchanging forces results in a data transfer of a single `float4` per (outer edge) particle, while exchanging positions and velocities would require exchanging twice as much data.

4.5.2 Computing during data exchange

Assuming data transfers have been minimized as discussed in the previous paragraph, the next step in an efficient multi-GPU implementation is to cover the data transfer latency by running computational kernels concurrently with the data transfer itself. This can be achieved as long as it is possible to efficiently launch computational kernels on a subset of the particle system (specifically, on the inner edge particles). It is then possible to first compute the new data on the inner edge particles, and then launch the kernel on the remaining (strictly inner) particles, while the inner edge data is sent to adjacent devices (and conversely the outer edge data is received from adjacent devices). This strategy allows optimal latency hiding, especially for the most computationally intensive kernels, provided all involved device are saturated. In GPUSPH, this is how we achieve nearly linear speedups in the number of devices [26], even when network transfers are involved in multi-node simulations [23].

4.5.3 Reference grid for domain decomposition

In our experience, multi-GPU also benefits from the use of the auxiliary grid that can be used for sorting (as described in Section 4.3) and for improved numerical accuracy (as will be described in Section 5.4): indeed, to improve the efficiency of data transfers, it is important that the sections of the arrays that need to be sent to adjacent devices are as consecutive as possible, since multiple small bursts are generally less efficient (both over the PCI Express bus and over the network) than larger data transfers.

With the auxiliary reference grid, this can be obtained by always splitting the domain at the cell level and computing the cell index by taking the inner/edge/outer relation into consideration (**Figure 4**). In GPUSPH this is achieved by reserving the two most significant bits of the cell index to indicate strictly inner cells (00), inner edge cells (01), outer edge cells (10), and strictly outer cells (11)—with the latter never actually used except in an optional global cell map. With this strategy, all strictly inner particles will be sorted first, followed by all inner edge particles, and finally by outer edge particles. Since outer edge particles will be sorted consecutively in memory, receiving data about them will be more efficient; similarly, sending inner edge data over will be made more efficient by the coalesced layout.

Note that this cell sorting strategy does not completely eliminate the need for multiple transfers; it does however help to reduce it significantly, especially when combined with linear cell indexing and the appropriate choice of order of dimensions for linearization. For this reason, GPUSPH offers a (compile-time) option to allow customization of this choice that in our experience can have performance benefits of up to 30%.

5. Numerical robustness

When the intent of GPGPU is to leverage the low-cost, high-performance ratio offered by consumer GPUs, a significant bottleneck in scientific applications is given by the limited (when not completely absent) support for double precision: since consumer GPUs are designed for video games and similar applications, where the highest rendering accuracy is not a requirement, the hardware is optimized for single-precision computation. Applications that need higher accuracy can thus follow one of the following strategies: use double-precision anyway, use soft extended precision (double-float, etc.), and rely on alternative algorithms that ensure a better utilization of the available precision.

Due to the high-performance cost (ratios as low as 1:32 compared to single precision, nearly completely defeating the benefits of the high performance of GPUs over CPUs), the use of double precision should be avoided whenever possible. If absolutely necessary, it should be restricted to parts of the code where it is essential. In all other cases, faster alternatives should be sought out. A possible solution is offered by double-float arithmetic, in which two single-precision values are used to provide higher accuracy [27, 28]: most operations will require between two and four hardware operation to complete, and the overall accuracy will generally be slightly lower than using actual double precision, but this can still be a good compromise between performance and accuracy when 64-bit floating-point has low or no support in hardware.

In many cases, it will be possible to avoid relying on extended precision by taking some care in the choice of algorithm used. In fact, the methods and algorithms that we will discuss momentarily can help improve the accuracy of an implementation regardless of the precision used: we would recommend their use even with double precision, since they always lead to more accurate results and in some cases (such as Horner's method) even higher performance.

5.1 Horner's method

Polynomial evaluation should always be done using Horner's method [29]. Any polynomial $a_n x^n + a_{n-1} x^{n-1} + \ldots + a_1 x + a_0$ can be written in the equivalent form

$$((\ldots((a_n x + a_{n-1})x + a_{n-2})x + \ldots)x + a_1)x + a_0.$$

When this second form is evaluated from the innermost to the outermost expression, better accuracy and performance can be achieved. Indeed, Horner's method is known to be optimal in that it requires the minimal number of additions and multiplications for the evaluation of the polynomial [30, 31], and given the widespread availability of fused multiply-add operations on modern hardware, every term can be computed with a higher accuracy and in a single cycle, making this evaluation method the fastest and most accurate for general polynomials.

5.2 Compensated and balanced summation

In many particle systems, the behavior of a particle is dictated by the influence of a local neighborhood: the total action on the central particle is then achieved by adding up the contributions from each neighboring particle. The number of contributions is frequently in the order of tens or hundreds and in some applications even more. The naive approach, which could be described algorithmically as

```
total_action=0;;
for (i=0; i<num_neighbors; ++i);
      total_action +=contribution_from_neighbor(i);
```

suffers from low accuracy: since each contribution adds a relative error in the order of the machine epsilon ε, the total relative error is in the order of the total number of contributions, $O(\varepsilon n)$ in the worst case (in practice, the error is typically $O(\varepsilon\sqrt{n})$ with the default round-to-nearest rounding mode).

This can be significantly improved by using a compensated summation algorithm, which can bring down the total relative error to order $O(1)$ (constant). The idea behind this class of algorithms is to keep track of the quantity that gets "lost" during a summation due to the finite precision. This is achieved by keeping two accumulators, the `sum` itself and a `correction`. The simplest form of compensated summation was popularized by Kahan [32], where the contribution from each new `term` is computed as shown in **Listing 5**.

The approach relies on the compiler not trying to do an algebraic simplification of the expressions for the temporary sum `t` and the `correction`, which may require disabling "fast-math" and the contraction of floating-point expressions.

The Kahan compensated summation algorithm works best when all terms in the summation are of similar or decreasing orders of magnitude but fail to take into account that the new term may be (significantly) larger in magnitude than the current running sum. To this end, Neumaier presented a variant [33], usually known as KBN (Kahan-Babuška-Neumaier), that takes into account the relative magnitude of the new `term` and the running sum when computing the correction (**Listing 6**). In contrast to Kahan's algorithm, the final sum is obtained by adding `sum` and `correction`. More details about balancing and compensated summation algorithms can be found in [34].

The main downside of KBN is the branching condition to compute the correction, which may reduce performance on GPU. The algorithm can be rewritten to be vector-friendly, as illustrated on the right in **Listing 6**, which makes use of the `select(a, b, c)` function and the component-by-component extension to the ternary operator `c ? b : a` defined, e.g., in OpenCL C. This form of KBN should only be chosen when profiling shows the branching to be a performance bottleneck, since the extra operations otherwise introduce higher latency in the summation.

Listing 5.
Kahan summation algorithm.

```
y=term - correction;             /* take into account what got lost previously */
t=sum + y;                       /* temporary sum: add the new term y */
correction=(t - sum) - y;        /* estimate what got lost adding the new term */
sum=t;                           /* actual new value of the summation */
```

Listing 6.
KBN (Kahan-Babuška-Neumaier) summation algorithm. Standard form (left) and possible vectorization (right).

```
t=sum + term;
if (abs(sum)>= abs(term)) {
    correction +=(sum - t)+term;
} else {
    correction +=(term - t)+sum;
}
sum=t;
```

```
t=sum + term;
cond=(abs(sum)>= abs(term));
sum_or_term=select(term, sum, cond);
term_or_sum=select(sum, term, cond);
correction +=(sum_or_term - t)+term_or_sum;
sum=t;
```

The downsides of compensated summation algorithms are higher storage requirements (the additional accumulator) and higher computational cost (Kahan, e.g., requires four times more operations compared to the standard summation). Compared to the use of double precision, the storage requirements are unchanged; the computational cost, however, is two (or more) times higher than the cost of double-precision on hardware that supports it at full frequency; on most consumer GPUs, however, the use of compensated summation can be up to eight times *faster* than the use of double precision.

Compensated summation algorithms can be used both locally, at the single kernel level, to improve the computation of the contributions for the next time step, and globally, across kernel launches, providing better accuracy for long-running simulations.

5.3 Vector norms and the `hypot` function

Computing the norm of a vector is a very frequent operation. In Euclidean metric, the norm is computed as the square root of the sum of the square of the components and thus requires `d` multiplications, `d-1` additions, and a square root. With the exception of very high dimensions, the final square root is frequently the most expensive operation as well as the least accurate.

The first step to improve both performance and accuracy is therefore to avoid taking the square root if possible. For example, when the vector is a distance and the objective is to compare distances, it is much faster (and accurate) to compare the squared distances (sum of the squares of the differences of the components) rather than the distances themselves. When the distance has to be compared against a reference length, it is cheaper to square the reference length than it is to take the square root in the distance computations.

A typical circumstance where one cannot avoid taking the square root is normalization of a vector, in which each component needs to be divided by the length of the vector; in some applications this is such a frequent (and slow) operation that fast, but less accurate implementations are used, such as the fast inverse square root [35] popularized by its use in id Software *Quake III: Arena* video game [36].

While games can afford to sacrifice accuracy for performance, this is not the case in scientific applications, for which a significant issue in vector normalization (and similar operations) is numerical stability: when the vector has components which are very close to zero, a naive computation of the norm may lead to underflow, potentially resulting in a final division by zero during normalization; conversely, very large components can lead to overflow of the inner summation before the root extraction.

The solution is to compute the norm using the hypot operator. The idea is to rewrite $\sqrt{a_0^2 + a_1^2 + \ldots + a_n^2}$ as $|a_0|\sqrt{1 + q_1^2 + \ldots + q_n^2}$ where $q_i = a_i/a_0$. In exact arithmetic the two expressions are equivalent, but with finite precision, the second expression is more accurate, assuming the values are sorted by magnitude (largest to smallest). The higher accuracy of hypot however comes at a significant computational cost, due to the additional division per component: even highly optimized implementations of hypot (such as the two-argument function available in the standard C library, in OpenCL C and in CUDA) can easily be as much as two orders of magnitude slower than the naive approach.

5.4 Local versus global position

A major difference between numerical methods such as finite differences and meshless methods such as smoothed particle hydrodynamics is that in the former case, there is no need to track the global position of each computational node, as this is defined algorithmically based on the (possibly adaptive) mesh size, and the internode distance is fixed and known in advance. Meshless methods, on the other hand, need to track the global position of each particle; due to the nonuniform distribution of floating-point values, the inter-particle distance (computed as the difference between the global position of the particles) will then have a higher precision near the origin of the domain and a lower precision the further away from the origin the particles are. When the ratio of the inter-particle distance to the domain size gets close to machine epsilon, this nonuniform accuracy may lead to artificial clustering of particles, an effect that is quite noticeable when using single precision to simulate very large domains with a very fine resolution (**Figure 5**).

While extending the precision for the global position is a possible solution [37], this only delays the problem and, as mentioned previously, may have a nontrivial computational cost. An alternative approach is to use a support, fixed grid with regular spacing and only track the position of each particle with respect to the center of the grid cell it belongs to [38]; distances to the other particles are obtained by correcting the distance between the grid cell centers and the local position difference (**Listing 7**). Absolute (global) positions are only reconstructed when necessary (e.g., when writing the results to disk).

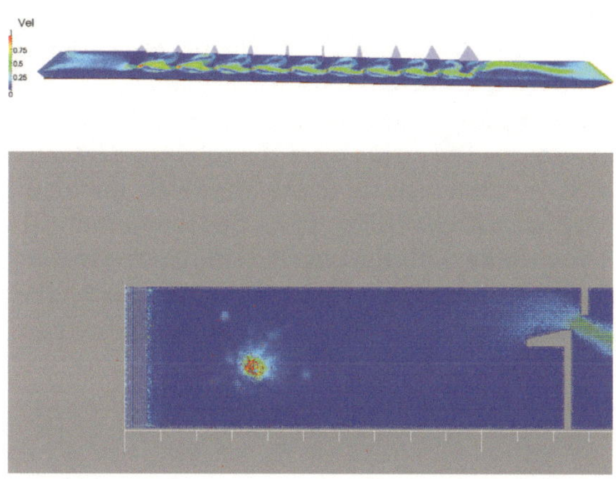

Figure 5.
Simulation of an 8-pool fish pass with GPUSPH before the introduction of uniform position precision. At high resolutions, spurious explosion due to insufficient precision near the domain edge can be observed.

Listing 7.
Computing particle distance with uniform precision using cell indices and local positions.

```
const float3 cell_size;                  /* global constant: cell size */
int3 our_cell, neib_cell;                /* (integer) coordinates of the cells */
float3 our_lpos, neib_lpos;              /* particle position wrt their cell center */
float3 dist_vec =                        /* particle distance, computed from the local
    (neib_cell - our_cell)*cell_size +      position difference and the cell center
    (neib_lpos - our_lpos);                 distance */
```

This approach doubles the storage requirement (e.g., in three dimensions, an additional `int3` is needed to describe the cell index, in addition to the local position stored in a `float3`), matching the requirement of the higher-precision type (e.g., storing global positions but using a `double3` per particle), with the additional benefit of uniform accuracy throughout the domain, and the possibility to support much larger domains, even larger than would be allowed with higher precision. If the overall number of cells is relatively low, storage requirements can be reduced by encoding the cell coordinates in less memory: for example, if the overall number of cells is less than 2^{32}, it is possible to store a linearized cell index in a single `unsigned int`. The support grid solution is particularly advantageous when the same grid (and linearized cell index) can also be used for neighbor search, as described in Section 4.3, and to improve the performance of multi-GPU simulations, as discussed in Section 4.5.

5.5 Relative and nondimensional quantities

A general rule to improve the numerical stability of most methods is to work in nondimensional form, i.e., to scale all quantities (length, time, mass, etc.) by some problem-specific scale factor related to the problem's characteristic numbers (e.g., the Reynold number in case of viscous flows), and rewrite the underlying equations in terms of the nondimensional quantities instead of using standard units.

Working with nondimensional quantities can lead to better accuracy by allowing fuller utilization of the range of the floating-point values, but additional steps can be taken to gain further accuracy. An example of this is the local coordinate system proposed in the previous paragraph that alone is sufficient to improve the energy conservation of GPUSPH by as much as four orders of magnitude [38], but the same principle can be extended to most quantities. The benefits are particularly high when the range of variation of the quantity itself is small.

For example, in the weakly compressible SPH formulation, the density ρ of the particles in a fluid is assumed to differ from the reference (at-rest) value ρ_o by at most a few percent. In nondimensional terms, the recommended approach would be to work with the *relative density* $RD = \rho/\rho_0$, but the numerical accuracy can be further improved by working with the *centered relative density* $\tilde{\rho} = \rho/\rho_o - 1$, which allows us to gain three or more digits of accuracy and to bring the absolute error in the computation of the neighbor contribution to the pressure part of the momentum equation from 10^{-7} down to 10^{-11} [38].

6. Flexibility

When setting forth to implement a new particle engine, important decisions have to be made concerning the general design of the system, particularly in reference to the scope and objectives. This is particularly important for particle system, due to the possible temptation to produce a "universal particle system engine" that could be extended to support any kind of particle system: a worthy objective, but in direct contrast with the need to have something useful and functional "right now." As a general rule, our recommendation is to start with a well-focused objective (e.g., a very specific formulation of a numerical method) and only extend/expand the objective for specific use cases.

The focus of the initial implementation of a particle system (as for any general application) should always be correctness over performance. This is true also when specifically targeting high-performance computing (e.g., when designing for a GPU implementation). There are however some important design aspects that can be kept in mind, with low implementation cost and high return of investment at later development stages, both in terms of code cleanliness and extensibility. We will present them in this section, showing how the complexity that comes with flexibility can be isolated to provide a cleaner interface and without sacrificing (runtime) performance.

6.1 Separation of roles

Implementations of particle systems can be characterized by three main roles: *management* (setup, teardown, data exchange, e.g., saving/visualization), *evolution* (abstract sequence of steps that describe a single iteration of the lifetime of the system), and *execution* (concrete functions and kernels for each individual step). Keeping these roles distinct from the beginning can provide a solid base for the growth of the implementation; for example, while at first the developer may focus on single GPU, a subsequent extension to multi-GPU can be achieved more easily at a later stage if the management and execution roles are delegated to separate classes, running on separate threads: typically, management is handled by the main thread, while the execution role will be delegated to a worker thread (which become multiple worker threads in the multi-GPU case).

Two approaches are then possible: assign the evolution role (i.e., the decisions about which steps to run next) to the manager thread or to the workers. The latter choice ("smart workers") has the advantage that the worker threads know what to do for every step, and this can be leveraged to reduce synchronization points; the downside is that unification tasks (such as global reductions and data exchange in the multi-node case) must be taken over by a specific worker, which creates an imbalance (since not all workers are created equal). Conversely, with "dumb workers," most commands become a synchronization point (which can become a performance bottleneck), but the manager thread can more easily subsume the unification tasks. Hybrid solutions are also possible, at the expense of a growing complexity in logic. Factoring out the (abstract description of the) evolution into its own class (in the object-oriented programming sense) can make it easier to transition from one implementation to the other.

6.1.1 Workers for hardware abstraction

Refactoring the execution role into a separate `Worker` class has several advantages. The most important, as mentioned above, is that having a separate `Worker` class provides a solid ground to expand the code to support multiple GPUs (with each `Worker` taking control of a separate device).

Additionally, with the correct design, wider hardware support can be implemented by making the `Worker` class itself an abstract class, implementing only the common code, such as the evolution logic in the case of smart workers, or the command dispatch table in the case of dumb workers. Derived classes would then implement the hardware-specific details such as the actual kernel execution or the host/device memory transfers. For example, one could have a `GPUWorker` for execution on GPU and a `CPUWorker` for execution on CPU [26]; the `GPUWorker` class itself could be further specialized in a `CUDAWorker` and an `OpenCLWorker`, when support for both APIs is desired.

6.2 The cost of variation

The complexity of the implementation of each individual step of the evolution loop in the particle system is directly related to the number of features offered; for example, some sections of the code may only be relevant when the fluid needs to interact with moving objects; or some particle types or particle data may only be present if specific options (e.g., an SPH formulation) are enabled; or it may be possible to choose between a faster but less accurate approach and a computationally more expensive, more accurate solution.

There are two main costs that come with providing multiple features (or variations thereof): an implementation cost (larger, more complex code to write) and a runtime cost. Both costs can be reduced with appropriate care in the design of the software. An optimal implementation should be designed in such a way that the runtime cost of a disabled feature matches the runtime cost had it not been implemented in the first place. For example, if the user runs an SPH simulation without any moving objects, then the runtime should be the same in an SPH implementation that does not support moving objects, and in an implementation that does support them, but that can detect (or can be told) that support for them is not needed. Likewise, the implementation of any additional feature should be as unobtrusive as possible, factored out into its own sets of functions. Luckily these two goals are not in conflict.

6.2.1 Managing buffers

One of the key aspects in supporting multiple variants for particle systems is correct buffer management. The objective is to support allocating all and only the (copies of the) buffers that are needed, correctly sized, in a unified manner (i.e., with the same interface on host and device). Moreover, we want to be able to pass around sets of buffers (e.g., the collection of all allocated buffers or a specific subset of them) to other parts of the code, in a way that minimizes both the actual copying of data and the detailed specification of which buffers belong to a set.

The approach we use in GPUSPH to solve this issue relies on two aspects: bitmask-based buffer naming and a set of classes that abstract buffer management, isolating the details of the individual buffer while still allowing the retrieval of all the necessary information, such as the data type, the number of elements, the kind of buffer (e.g., host or device), etc.

Bitmask-based buffer naming relies on using an appropriate set of values (defined with either `#define`s or an `enum`) to refer to the buffers, on the condition that each (symbolic) buffer name corresponds to an individual bit. These symbolic buffer names are used to refer to buffers in most of the host code, with the exceptions of the classes and functions that require access to the actual corresponding data pointers (i.e., the lowest level of implementation of the `GPUWorker`). An example of this is shown in **Listing 8**, which needs to be paired with an appropriate `BufferList` class such that, given `BufferList buffers`, we can get the array of positions as `buffers.getData<BUFFER_POS>()`.

With each symbolic name associated to a separate buffer, it is possible to combine them into an expression to refer to multiple buffers at once. For example,

Listing 8.
Buffer as member variables (left) versus buffer symbolic names (right).

```
float4 *bufferPos;
int *bufferNeibs;
float2 *bufferTau[3]; /* stress tensor */
```

```
#define BUFFER_POS (1U<<0)
#define BUFFER_NEIBS (1U<<1)
#define BUFFER_TAU (1U<<2)
```

BUFFER_POS | BUFFER_VEL would indicate a collection of buffers holding both the positions and the velocity. This is particularly useful in conjunction with the "dumb worker" approach, because it allows most commands given by the Manager thread to the Workers to have a syntax such as

```
doCommand(COMMAND_NAME, BUFFER_R1 | BUFFER_R2 | ...,
   BUFFER_W1 | BUFFER_W2 | ...);
```

where the list of input and output buffers for the command are given as single parameters by doing a binary OR of the symbolic buffer names.

In languages such as C++, the use of symbolic names (with or without the bitmask property) also allows static knowledge about the buffer properties to be encoded into "traits" structure that can be used to evince information about the buffers at compile time, as exemplified in **Listing 9**. This allows developers to programmatically determine the element type of a buffer as BufferTraits <symbolic_name>::element_type, which can be used in our BufferList class to make sure that when requesting a specific array, we get a pointer of the correct type and BufferTraits<symbolic_name>::num_buffers to determine how many components the buffer has (e.g., in this example we model a symmetric 3×3 tensor, which has six components, as a collection of three float2 buffers).

The management of the actual data is handled with different layers of abstraction. We use an AbstractBuffer class to describe the interface shared by all buffers, regardless of content or type; the interface presents (pure virtual) methods for operations such as allocations and deallocation of data, as well as a way to return a "generic" pointer to the data itself (as a void*, since no type information is available in AbstractBuffer).

The next layer can be implemented as a GenericBuffer class template that depends on the data type and number of components of the buffer, so that GenericBuffer<float2, 3>would be able to handle storage and typed access to per-particle symmetric tensor data (encoded in three float2 per particle).

Listing 9.
Example declaration of a BufferTraits structure and its specializations for some named buffers, declaring their data type and multiplicity.

```
template<int Buffer> struct BufferTraits;

template<> struct BufferTraits<BUFFER_POS>
{
    typedef float4 element_type;
    enum {num_buffers=1};
};
```

```
template<> struct BufferTraits<BUFFER_NEIBS>
{
    typedef int element_type;
    enum {num_buffers=1};
};
template<> struct BufferTraits<BUFFER_TAU>
{
    typedef float2 element_type;
    enum {num_buffers=3};
};
```

Since we can derive element types and number of components from the buffer traits, our Buffer class template can simply derive from the appropriate GenericBuffer:

```
template<flag_t Key>
class Buffer : public GenericBuffer<
      BufferTraits<Key>::element_type,
      BufferTraits<Key>::num_buffers>
{ /* other specializations, as necessary */ };
```

Note that the Buffer class template still does not have any actual allocation logic: its only purpose is to provide the correct base class for the named properties of each particle (e.g., position, velocity, etc.). The allocation logic is delegated to derived classes such as HostBuffer (that would use malloc/free or new/delete), CUDABuffer (using cudaMalloc/cudaFree), and CLBuffer (using clCreateBuffer/clReleaseMemObject).

Finally, a collection of buffers is managed by a BufferList that maps symbolic names to the concrete class implementing the buffer with the specific symbolic name.

Since different variants of a particle system will instance different subsets of all possible buffers, the mapping will in general be sparse, and it is therefore better to use a dictionary type such as std::map (or language equivalent) to implement it. This is particularly true for the bitmask choice of symbolic names. Moreover, since each symbolic name maps to a buffer with a different data type, the mapping will generally be between symbolic names and AbstractBuffers. Downcasting to the correct Buffer<symbolic_name> type can be done in specific template methods, where the symbolic name is known as compile type. Our BufferList class, for example, exposes a template getData method that returns a pointer of the correct type for the given symbolic name, again using the buffer traits to deduce it; some example of its usage are illustrated further on.

In general, a single instance of a running particle system will have multiple BufferLists: it may have one to hold the data on host (e.g., for saving or visualization) and one on device to hold the data for the running simulation; on device, it might have more than one, separating read/write copies of each buffer, or to hold the data for different parts of the particle system (e.g., a BufferList for fluid particle data, a BufferList for boundary particle data); it may also have one (or more) BufferLists to hold all of the available data for the particle system and separate smaller BufferLists with a selection of the data when passing it to individual kernels, depending on the approach used.

6.2.2 Handling options combinatorial growth

As the number of options offered to the end user of a particle system grows, there is a consequent explosion in the number of possible valid combinations that need to be supported, which results in competing needs between the opportunity (for performance reasons) for their compile-time implementation, and the associated resource consumption at compile time when runtime selection of the specific option is offered.

(At some point of time, compiling all of the combinations of simulation parameters offered by GPUSPH took several hours, occupying several gigabytes of memory and producing a binary with around 3000 variants of the main computational kernels overall.)

There are two possible solutions to this issue. The simplest solution, which is currently used in GPUSPH, is to push down the compile-time selection to the user: the setup of the user simulation is done via a source file where all the compile-time parameters must be selected. When the user simulation setup is compiled, only the specific combination of parameters will be enabled and compiled for. An alternative solution is to rely on the specific possibility offered with GPU programming, to compile the device code at runtime. This feature has always been available with OpenCL (in fact, OpenCL *requires* runtime compilation of the device code), and it has been recently made available in CUDA via the NVRTC library.

The main downside of the compile-time selection is that the software must always be distributed in source form, with several implications in terms of user-friendliness and maintenance. Downsides for runtime compilation include the limited support for older version of CUDA, when relying on this proprietary solution, and the potential time loss at the beginning of each execution (which may or may not be offset by any caching the runtime compilation engine might do).

On the other hand, runtime compilation of the device code allows an even wider range of aspects to be implemented at compile time (on the device side), which may allow even stronger compiler optimizations. For example, global simulation parameters that are constant throughout a simulation are often stored in the device constant memory at the beginning of the simulation; even though access to constant memory is quite efficient, inlining the constants can be even more efficient, and this can be achieved exploiting runtime compilation, by replacing the upload of the constants to the device with appropriate `#define` in the runtime-compiled device code.

6.2.3 C++ SFINAE versus C preprocessors for compile-time specialization

Implementing multiple variations of a kernel (or function used by a kernel) is generally nontrivial, as the functions may have different sets of parameters and different private variables and may operate differently even on data that is present in all or most of them. The objective is therefore to isolate the variant-specific parts from the common parts, avoiding code repetition.

When using runtime compilation for the device code and a C-based language such as OpenCL C, the only way to achieve this is to fence nonrelevant parts of the code with appropriate preprocessor directives, as illustrated in **Listing 10** (left). Code fencing can be factored out, and sometimes reduced, by collecting data into conditional structures and refactoring computations into conditional functions; the resulting code is slightly more verbose (**Listing 10**, right), but the optional features are better isolated, improving the maintainability of the code.

Note that the conditional structure in this example cannot be extended to the kernel parameters and private variables itself, due to the impossibility for global array addresses to be member of structures shared between host and device, which further limits the possibility to initialize the conditional parts of the private variable structure with appropriate conditional functions. (This is a limitation of OpenCL C; alternative solutions are possible using the Shared Virtual Memory feature introduced in OpenCL 2.0 and supported by some implementations as an extension on older versions of the standard.)

When the device code can be written in C++ and global arrays pointers are made available in the same form to both the host and device (e.g., with CUDA), the language itself provides powerful meta-programming techniques that can be leveraged to eliminate the need for a preprocessor, allowing multiple specialized implementations to coexist.

Listing 10.
Code fencing for optional components in the case of runtime device code compilation: inline approach (left) and refactored approach with code isolation (right).

```
kernel void some_kernel(
    global const float4 * restrict posArray,
    global const float4 * restrict velArray,
#ifdef HAS_XSPH
    global float4 * restrict xsphArray
#endif
#ifdef HAS_STRESS_TENSOR
    global float4 * restrict stressTensor4,
    global float4 * restrict stressTensor2,
#endif
    global float4 * restrict forces)
{
    /* common private variables go here */
#ifdef HAS_XSPH
    /* XSPH private variables go here */
#endif
#ifdef HAS_STRESS_TENSOR
    /* stress tensor private variables go here */
#endif
    /* common computations go here */
#ifdef HAS_XSPH
    /* XSPH computations go here */
#endif
#ifdef HAS_STRESS_TENSOR
    /* stress tensor computations go here */
#endif
}
```

```
struct private_vars {
    /* common private variables */
#ifdef HAS_XSPH
    /* XSPH private variables */
#endif
#ifdef HAS_STRESS_TENSOR
    /* stress tensor private variables */
#endif
};
void process_common(struct private_vars *priv)
{/* common computations here */}
void process_xsph(struct private_vars * priv)
#ifdef HAS_XSPH
{/* XSPH computations go here */}
#else
{} /* intentionally left blank */
#endif
void process_stress_tensor(
    struct private_vars * priv)
#ifdef HAS_STRESS_TENSOR
{/* stress tensor computations go here */}
#else
{} /* intentionally left blank */
#endif
kernel void some_kernel(
    global const float4 * restrict posArray,
    global const float4 * restrict velArray,
#ifdef HAS_XSPH
    global float4 * restrict xsphArray
#endif
#ifdef HAS_STRESS_TENSOR
    global float4 * restrict stressTensor4,
    global float4 * restrict stressTensor2,
#endif
    global float4 * restrict forces)
{
    struct private_vars priv;
    /* initialize common part of priv */
#ifdef HAS_XSPH
    /* initialize XSPH part of priv */
#endif
#ifdef HAS_STRESS_TENSOR
    /* initialize stress tensor part of priv */
#endif
    process_common(&priv);
    process_xsph(&priv);
    process_stress_tensor(&priv);
}
```

Conditional structures and functions in C++ can be implemented by using templates and the meta-programming feature of the language known as SFINAE (substitution failure is not an error) to select function specializations based on any combination of (compile-time) properties of their parameters. The approach we show requires two building blocks that are available in the standard library since C++11 (and can even be implemented in older C++ versions) and a special `empty` structure template.

The first building block is a structure template.

```
template<bool B, typename T, typename F>struct conditional;
```

such that `conditional<somecondition, SomeType, SomeOtherType>::type` corresponds to `SomeType` when `somecondition` is true and to `SomeOtherType` when the condition is false. This is part of C++11 and can be also defined in previous versions of the standard [39].

The purpose of the `empty` structure template is to "absorb" any type, construct from anything, and otherwise be empty. Using C++11 variadic templates for the constructor, it can be implemented as.

```
template<typename T>struct empty {
   template<typename U...>empty(U... args) {}
   };
```

In older versions of C++, the single variadic template constructor must to be replaced with multiple constructor templates, each taking a separate number of arguments.

With these building blocks, we can define our conditional structure support type, relying on the C++11 `using` template directive:

```
template<bool B, typename T>
using cond_struct=typename
      conditional< B, T, empty<T> >::type;
```

When forced to use older C++ versions, something similar but less robust can be implemented with a macro such as.

```
#define COND_STRUCT(cond, ...) \
      typename conditional<cond, __VA_ARGS__, \
         empty<__VA_ARGS> >::type
```

A structure with optional members can then be defined by defining multiple structures grouping each set of optional members and then defining the main structure as derived from all substructures, each wrapped in their own `cond_struct<>`, as illustrated in **Listing 11**. We see how the individual groups of members for the final structure are refactored into simpler structures, carrying their own initialization information. We also see why the empty structure needs to be a template: if this was not the case, and both XSPH and the stress tensor computation were disabled, the kernel parameters structure would have `empty` as a base class twice, which is not allowed by the standard; with our template approach, the two empty base classes are now formally distinct types: `empty<xsph_kernel_params>` and `empty<stress_kernel_params>`. The sample code also shows the advantage of the `BufferList` class described previously and its typed buffer access methods. On the device side, we can use the same approach for the private variables of the kernel (**Listing 12**).

Finally, we need to define the individual process functions. For this, we need separate overloads depending on whether the `priv` structure has the specific members or not. One way to achieve this is to make all functions depend on the same template parameters as the structure, but when there are many parameters, this becomes quite complex and hard to maintain and extend, since every additional parameter will require a change in all the functions that access

Listing 11.
Conditional structures with C++ applied to kernel parameters: definition of the optional members (left) and definition of the conditional structure template including them (right).

```
struct common_kernel_params {
    const float4 * restrict posArray;
    const float4 * restrict velArray;
    float4 * restrict forcesArray;

    common_kernel_params(BufferList& buffers)
: posArray(buffers.getData<BUFFER_POS>())
, velArray(buffers.getData<BUFFER_VEL>())
, forcesArray(buffers.getData<BUFFER_FORCES>())
    {}
};

struct xsph_kernel_params {
    float4 * restrict xsphArray;

    xsph_kernel_params(BufferList& buffers)
: xsphArray(buffers.getData<BUFFER_XSPH>())
    {}
};

struct stress_kernel_params {
    float4 * restrict stressTensor4,
    float4 * restrict stressTensor2,
    stress_kernel_params(BufferList& buffers)
: stressTensor4(buffers.getData<BUFFER_TAU4>())
, stressTensor2(buffers.getData<BUFFER_TAU2>())
    {}
};
```

```
template<
    /* actual template parameters */
bool needs_xsph, bool needs_stress_tensor,
/* pseudo-template parameters,
  used to give simpler names to
  conditional structure members */
  typename optional_xsph=
cond_struct<needs_xsph, xsph_kernel_params>,
  typename optional_stress =
cond_struct<needs_stress_tensor,
  stress_kernel_params>
>
struct kernel_params
  : common_kernel_params
  , optional_xsph
  , optional_stress
{
  /* These static variables allow compile-time
    knowledge about the parameters used
    for the specific instantiation
    of the template */
  static const bool has_xsph=needs_xsph;
  static const bool has_stress=
needs_stress_tensor;

  kernel_params(BufferList& buffers)
    : common_kernel_params(buffers)
    , optional_xsph(buffers)
    , optional_stress(buffers)
  {}
};
```

the structure, regardless of whether the additional parameter actually has an impact.

A simple way is to make the functions into templates depending on a single parameter (the arbitrary type of the structure passed), and then make overloads based on specific properties of the actual structure that gets passed. This can be achieved by means of enable_if, a structure template declared as.

```
template<bool B, typename T=void> enable_if;
```

which is such that enable_if<condition, SomeType>::type is SomeType when the condition is true and an error otherwise. Due to the SFINAE principle, when the compiler is looking for the overload of a function to use, it will discard (without errors) the overloads which result in an error and automatically select the one which does not result in an error. Additionally, if SomeType is omitted, void is implied, which can simply the syntax. Again, this template is provided by the standard library in C++11 and can be implemented in older version of C++ [40].

To further simplify the syntax, we assume that C++11 is available and we can define:

```
template<bool B, typename T=void>
using enable_if_t=typename enable_if<B, T>::type;
```

(which is pre-defined in C++14).

Listing 12.
Conditional structures with C++ applied to private function variables: definitions of the optional members (left) and definition of the conditional structure template including them (right).

```
struct common_kernel_priv {
    /* common variables become members
       of this structure */
    common_kernel_priv(
       common_kernel_params const& params)
    {/* initialize the variables
       from the parameters */}
};

struct xsph_kernel_priv {
    /* XSPH-specific variables become members
       of this structure */
    xsph_kernel_priv(x
       sph_kernel_params const& params)
    {/* typically, feature-specific variables
       will be initialized from
       feature-specific kernel parameters */}
};

struct stress_kernel_priv {
    /* Stress-tensor specific variables
       become members of this structure */
    stress_kernel_priv(
       stress_kernel_params const& params)
    {/* typically, feature-specific variables
       will be initialized from
       feature-specific kernel parameters */}
};
```

```
template<
    bool needs_xsph, bool needs_stress_tensor,
    typename optional_xsph =
cond_struct<needs_xsph, xsph_kernel_priv>,
    typename optional_stress =
cond_struct<needs_stress_tensor,
    stress_kernel_priv>
>
struct kernel_priv
: common_kernel_priv
, optional_xsph
, optional_stress
{
    /* These static variables allow compile-time
       knowledge about the parameters used for
       the specific instantiation of
       the template */
    static const bool has_xsph=needs_xsph;
    static const bool has_stress=
needs_stress_tensor;

    kernel_priv(kernel_params<needs_xsph,
needs_stress_tensor> const& params)
       : common_kernel_priv(params)
       , optional_xsph(params)
       , optional_stress(params)
    {}
};
```

The processing functions can then be defined as in **Listing 13**, with separate overloads made available based on compile-time properties of the argument. The kernel structure becomes very simple (**Listing 14**): all of the complexity has been delegated to specific (sub)structures and functions, and we have a guarantee that each specialized version of the kernel will only contain the code and variables that are pertinent to its functionality.

Listing 13.
Function specialization with overloads based on argument properties with enable-if in CUDA.

```
/* process_xsph is defined differently,
   depending on whether XSPH is enabled or not;
   we check for this based on the static const
   has_xsph member of the priv structure:
   this will always be present, and it will be
   true or false depending on whether
   XSPH was enabled */
template<typename Priv>
__device__ enable_if_t<Priv::has_xsph>
void process_xsph(Priv& priv)
{/* XSPH computations here */}

template<typename Priv>
__device__ enable_if_t<not Priv::has_xsph>
void process_xsph(Priv& priv)
{} /* intentionally left blank */
```

```
/* Similarly for the stress tensor,
using has_stress */
template<typename Priv>
__device__ enable_if_t<Priv::has_stress>
void process_stress_tensor(Priv& priv)
{/* stress tensor computations here */}

template<typename Priv>
__device__ enable_if_t<not Priv::has_stress>
void process_stress_tensor(Priv& priv)
{} /* intentionally left blank */

/* The common code needs no special treatment */
__device__ void
process_common(common_priv& priv)
{/* common computations here */}
```

Listing 14.
Kernel structure after isolation of the optional components.

```
template<
    bool needs_xsph, bool needs_stress,          /* template parameters for the kernel */
    typename Params =                            /* shorthand for the kernel parameters struct */
kernel_params<needs_xsph, needs_stress_tensor>,
    typename Priv =                              /* shorthand for the kernel private variables */
kernel_priv<needs_xsph, needs_stress_tensor>
>
__global__ void some_kernel(Params params)       /* kernel signature */
{
    /* initialize both common and optional private
    variables here */
    Priv priv(params);
    /* run common and optional parts of the code */
    process_common(priv);
    process_xsph(priv);
    process_stress_tensor(priv);
}
```

Listing 15.
Runtime switch to call the appropriate compile-time kernel specialization.

```
if (opt_xsph && opt_stress) some_kernel<<<...>>>(kernel_params<true, true>(buffers));
else if (opt_xsph && !opt_stress) some_kernel<<<...>>>(kernel_params<true, false>(buffers));
else if (!opt_xsph && opt_stress) some_kernel<<<...>>>(kernel_params<false, true>(buffers));
else if (!opt_xsph && !opt_stress) some_kernel<<<...>>>(kernel_params<false, false>(buffers));
```

Runtime selection of the variant of the kernel to be used can be achieved with simple conditionals (**Listing 15**). However, when the number of conditionals is large, this can be rather bothersome to write; more compact and efficient solutions to the runtime switch are possible, using the meta-programming techniques presented in [41].

When using C macros, the multiple specialized variants of the kernel and related structures and functions cannot coexist in the same compilation unit (since C does not support overloading or templates), making runtime selection of the compile-time variant impossible: a single specific instance must be selected when the device code is compiled; on the upside, one would generally use C when using OpenCL C, for which the device code is compiled at application runtime, as discussed in the previous section.

In terms of syntax, the only significant downside of the SFINAE approach is that the signature needs to be repeated for every specialization, in contrast to the C macro approach, for which we only need one signature, and each implementation is fenced by `#if/#elif/#else/#endif`. This could be avoided using the C++17 feature `if constexpr`, but support for it in device code is still missing.

7. Conclusions

Particle systems are a fundamental aspect of many applications and numerical methods. By their own nature, they benefit from the massively parallel stream processing architecture of modern GPUs, but naive implementations can easily encounter pitfalls that can limit the full exploitation of the hardware.

While hardware vendors go to great lengths to support more liberal coding, the software can—and should—be designed to leverage the natural programming model of the hardware, and we have provided several insights on how the particle systems can be designed to fit better with the requirements of optimal GPU usage. We also presented a few simple ideas that, when taken into consideration during an initial implementation, can make future extensions much easier. Many of the suggestions we provide can also be of general interest beyond the implementation of particle systems.

We have stressed the importance of the choice to the correct approach in dealing with the potentially severe limitations in the numerical robustness of the implementation, due to the restricted accuracy and precision of the single-precision floating-point format which GPUs are optimized for. While many of the techniques we have presented are not new (some going as far back as the nineteenth century), in our experience they have surprisingly limited adoption; we hope that our discussion of their usefulness in this context will lead to higher awareness of the possibilities they offer. We dislike the adoption of higher-precision data types as a solution to the issue, not only because of the performance implications on consumer hardware, but as a philosophical objection to waste: why use the wrong numerical approach, *wasting* the additional precision granted by double precision, when the correct approach can make single precision sufficient? We do understand the need for the extended precision requirements in many applications, and we are sure that our reminiscence of classical solutions to better accuracy can benefit them as well, particularly since support for even higher-precision data types is nearly nonexistent in hardware (with the possible exception of the IBM POWER9 support for IEEE-754-compliant 128-bit floating-point formats) and especially on GPUs.

Author details

Giuseppe Bilotta[1*], Vito Zago[1] and Alexis Hérault[2]

1 Istituto Nazionale di Geofisica e Vulcanologia, Sezione di Catania, Italy

2 Conservatoire National des Arts et Métiers, Laboratoire Modélisation mathématique et numérique, Paris, France

*Address all correspondence to: giuseppe.bilotta@ingv.it

References

[1] Reeves WT. Particle systems—A technique for modeling a class of fuzzy objects. ACM Transactions on Graphics. 1983;**2**(2):91-108. DOI: 10.1145/357318.357320

[2] Paramount. Star Trek II: The Wrath of Khan [film]. 1982

[3] Unity Technologies. Particle Systems. In: Unity User Manual v2018.2 [Internet]. 2018. Available from: https://docs.unity3d.com/Manual/index.html [Accessed: July 18, 2018]

[4] Monaghan JJ. Smoothed particle hydrodynamics and its diverse applications. Annual Review of Fluid Mechanics. 2012;**44**:323-346. DOI: 10.1146/annurev-fluid-120710-101220

[5] Chen JS, Liu WK, Hillman MC, Chi SW, Lian Y, Bessa MA. Reproducing kernel particle method for solving partial differential equations. In: Stein E, Borst R, Hughes TK, editors. Encyclopedia of Computational Mechanics. 2nd ed. Chichester, UK: Wiley; 2017. DOI: 10.1002/9781119176817.ecm2104

[6] Tiwari S, Kuhnert J. Finite pointset method based on the projection method for simulations of the incompressible Navier-Stokes equations. In: Griebel M, Schweitzer MA, editors. Meshfree Methods for Partial Differential Equations. Lecture Notes in Computational Science and Engineering. Vol. 26. Berlin, Heidelberg: Springer; 2003

[7] Bićanić N. Discrete element methods. In: Stein E, Borst R, Hughes TK, editors. Encyclopedia of Computational Mechanics. Chichester, UK: Wiley; 2017. DOI: 10.1002/0470091355.ecm006.pub2

[8] Kennedy J, Eberhart RC. Particle swarm optimization. In: Proceedings of ICNN'95—International Conference on Neural Networks; November 27– December 1, 1995; 2002. pp. 1942-1948. DOI: 10.1109/ICNN.1995.488968

[9] Stone JE, Phillips JC, Freddolino PL, Hardy DJ, Trabuco LG, Schulten K. Accelerating molecular modeling applications with graphics processors. Journal of Computational Chemistry. 2007;**28**:2618-2640. DOI: 10.1002/jcc.20829

[10] Richmond P. Template driven agent based modelling and simulation with CUDA. In: Hwu WM, editor. GPU Computing Gems Emerald Edition. Boston, USA: Morgan Kaufmann; 2011

[11] Richmond P, Walker D, Coakley S, Romano D. High performance cellular level agent-based simulation with FLAME for the GPU. Briefings in Bioinformatics. 2013;**11**(3):334-347. DOI: 10.1093/bib/bbp073

[12] Vuduc R, Choi J. A brief history and introduction to GPGPU. In: Shi X, Kindratenko V, Yang C, editors. Modern Accelerator Technologies for Geographic Information Science. Boston, MA: Springer; 2013. DOI: 10.1007/978-1-4614-8745-6_2

[13] Hérault A, Bilotta G, Dalrymple RA. SPH on GPU with CUDA. Journal of Hydraulic Research. 2010;**48**(Extra Issue):74-79. DOI: 10.1080/00221686.2010.9641247

[14] Bilotta G. GPU Implementation and Validation of Fully Three-Dimensional Multi-Fluid SPH Models. Rapporto Tecnico. 2014:292 INGV. Available from: http://istituto.ingv.it/images/collane-editoriali/rapporti%20tecnici/rapporti-tecnici-2014/rapporto292.pdf [Accessed: September 05, 2018]

[15] Bilotta G, Hérault A, Cappello A, Ganci G, Del Negro C. GPUSPH: a

smoothed particle hydrodynamics model for the thermal and rheological evolution of lava flows. In: Harris AJL, De Groeve T, Garel F, Carn SA, editors. Detecting, Modelling and Responding to Effusive Eruptions. Geological Society, London. 2016;426. DOI: 10.1144/SP426.24. Special Publications

[16] Zago V, Bilotta G, Hérault A, Dalrymple RA, Fortuna L, Cappello A, et al. Semi-implicit 3D SPH on GPU for lava flows. Journal of Computational Physics. 2018;**375**:854-870

[17] Zago V, Bilotta G, Cappello A, Dalrymple RA, Fortuna L, Ganci G, et al. Preliminary validation of lava benchmark tests on the GPUSPH particle engine. Annals of Geophysics. 2018;**61**. In Press

[18] GPUSPH v4.1 [Internet]. Available from: http://www.gpusph.org/ [Accessed: September 05, 2018]

[19] Khronos OpenCL Working Group. The OpenCL™ Specification [Internet]. 2018. Available from: https://www.khronos.org/registry/OpenCL/ [Accessed: September 05, 2018]

[20] NVIDIA. CUDA C Programming Guide [Internet]. 2018. Available from: https://docs.nvidia.com/cuda/ [Accessed: September 05, 2018]

[21] Green S. Particle Simulation Using CUDA. NVIDIA Corporation Whitepaper. 2010. Available from: http://developer.download.nvidia.com/assets/cuda/files/particles.pdf [Accessed: September 05, 2018]

[22] Bédorf J, Gaburov E, Portegies Zwart P. A sparse octree gravitational N-body code that runs entirely on the GPU processor. Journal of Computational Physics. 2012;**231**(7): 2825-2839. DOI: 10.1016/j.jcp.2011.12.024

[23] Rustico E, Jankowski JA, Hérault A, Bilotta G, Del Negro C. Multi-GPU, multi-node SPH implementation with arbitrary domain decomposition. In: Proceedings of the 9th SPHERIC Workshop; March 2014; Paris; 2014. pp. 127-133

[24] Burtscher M, Pingali K. Chapter 6: An efficient CUDA implementation of the tree-based Barnes Hut N-body. In: GPU Computing Gems Emerald Edition. Boston, USA: Morgan Kaufmann; 2011. pp. 75-92. DOI: 10.1016/B978-0-12-384988-5.00006-1

[25] Morton GM. A computer oriented geodetic data base; and a new technique in file sequencing. IBM Technical Report; 1966

[26] Rustico E, Bilotta G, Hérault A, Del Negro C, Gallo G. Advances in multi-GPU smoothed particle hydrodynamics simulations. IEEE Transactions on Parallel and Distributed Systems. 2012; **25**(1):43-52. DOI: 10.1109/TPDS.2012.340

[27] Li XS, Demmel JW, Bailey DH, Henry G, Hida Y, Iskandar J, et al. Design, implementation and testing of extended and mixed precision BLAS. ACM Transactions on Mathematical Software. 2002;**28**(2):152-205. DOI: 10.1145/567806.567808

[28] Colberg PH, Höfling F. Highly accelerated simulations of glassy dynamics using GPUs: Caveats on limited floating-point precision. Computer Physics Communications. 2011;**182**:1120-1129. DOI: 10.1016/j.cpc.2011.01.009

[29] Horner WG. A new method of solving numerical equations of all orders, by continuous approximation. Philosophical Transactions of the Royal Society of London. 1819;**109**:308-335. JSTOR: http://www.jstor.org/stable/107508

[30] Ostrowski AM. On two problems in abstract algebra connected with Horner's rule. In: von Mises R, editor. Studies in Mathematics and Mechanics. New York, USA: Academic Press; 2013. pp. 40-48. DOI: 10.1016/B978-1-4832-3272-0.50010-7

[31] Pan VY. Methods of computing values of polynomials. Russian Mathematical Surveys. 1966;**21**(1): 105-136. DOI: 10.1070/RM1966v021n01ABEH004147

[32] Kahan WM. Further remarks on reducing truncation errors. Communications of the ACM. 1964; **8**(1):40. DOI: 10.1145/363707.363723

[33] Neumaier A. Rundungsfehleranalyse einiger Verfahren zur Summation endlicher Summen. Zeitschrift für Angewandte Mathematik und Mechanik. 1974;**54**: 39-51. DOI: 10.1002/zamm.19740540106

[34] Klein A. A generalized Kahan-Babuška-Summation-algorithm. Computing. 2006;**76**(3–4):279-293. DOI: 10.1007/s00607-005-0139-x

[35] Blinn JF. Floating-point tricks. IEEE Computer Graphics and Applications. 1997;**17**(4):80-84. DOI: 10.1109/38.595279

[36] id Software. Quake III: Arena [Video Game]; 1999

[37] Domínguez JM, Crespo AJC, Barreiro A, Rogers BD, Gómez-Gesteira M. Efficient implementation of double precision in GPU computing to simulate realistic cases with high resolution. In: Proceedings of the 9th SPHERIC Workshop; March 2014; Paris; 2014. pp. 140-145

[38] Hérault A, Bilotta G, Dalrymple RA. Achieving the best accuracy in an SPH implementation. In: Proceedings of the 9th SPHERIC Workshop; March 2014; Paris; 2014. pp. 134-139

[39] cppreference. std::conditional [Internet]. 2018. Available from: https://en.cppreference.com/w/cpp/types/conditional [Accessed: September 05, 2018]

[40] cppreference. std::enable_if [Internet]. 2018. Available from: https://en.cppreference.com/w/cpp/types/enable_if [Accessed: September 05, 2018]

[41] Langr D, Tvrdík P, Dytrych T, Draayer JP. Fake run-time selection of template arguments in C++. In: Furia CA, Nanz S, editors. Objects, Models, Components, Patterns. TOOLS 2012. Lecture Notes in Computer Science. Vol. 7304. Berlin, Heidelberg: Springer; 2012. DOI: 10.1007/978-3-642-30561-0_11